CW01508649

THE
LOST ART
OF PLAYING
GOLF

Reconnect with the game you fell in love with

By Gary Nicol and Karl Morris

From the authors of the Amazon best-seller The Lost Art of Putting

lostartofgolf.com

About Sports Publications
Sports Publications are specialist golf publishers across magazines, books and digital formats.
They publish: National Club Golfer, Lady Golfer, NCG Top 100s, Society Golf Guide, The Golf Club Manager, Great Golf in England and BIGGA's Your Course as well as **nationalclubgolfer.com, lady-golfer.com** and several external titles.

The Lost Art of Playing Golf was edited by Dan Murphy, content director at Sports Publications.

The illustrations were drawn by Pete Swaine.

Published in 2019 in Great Britain. All rights reserved.
Published by Sports Publications Limited,
2 Arena Park, Leeds, LS17 9BF.
www.sports-publications.com
@SPPublications

ISBN: 978-1-9162106-0-8

CONTENTS

FOREWORD

By Rudy Duran, Tiger Woods' first coach

THE first I saw of Tiger Woods was when his mother, Tida, brought him to me at Heartwell Golf Park in Long Beach, California.

Heartwell is an 18-hole, par-3 course where I worked as one of the golf professionals.

Tida wanted to know if Tiger could be part of my junior programme and would I coach him. Tiger was four years old at the time and could barely see over the pro shop counter. I said we'd go to the driving range where I could see Tiger hit some balls.

I teed up four balls for him. He took out his cut-down 2 1/2 wood and proceeded to hit four perfect drives about 60 yards with a little bit of draw.

I said: "Wow – he can play here anytime and I would love to help with his game."

I knew at that moment that Tiger was special.

What I didn't know was how much I would learn from Tiger and that I was actually signing up to be the student.

I became a golf professional in 1971. I tried my hand at tournament golf from 1976 to 1978 with little success. I could hit the ball great in all areas but my scoring was always weak.

During those years of full-time golf I thought that if I just had the correct formula of positions I would always shoot low scores.

Well, that never happened. Hitting the ball well on the driving range and shooting low scores on the golf course are not the same thing.

I actually became the expert on what I was doing wrong when I needed to be the expert on my good shots and what I did well.

When Tiger and I would get together he would practise with me on the practice area and on the golf course.

We never spent much time talking about what was wrong.

It's more fun to celebrate our success. We would hit chip and pitch shots with different trajectories. High ones, low ones, shots that stopped, shots that ran out.

He just loved to create different golf shots. He wanted to know how to make the ball fly in different ways so he could score lower. He wouldn't have known about the position at the top of the swing or when he set his wrists.

If he wanted to learn a certain shape of shot I offered some suggestions as to how the club might feel through the ball to affect the flight of the shot.

Our sessions were all about creating an environment of fun, learning and remembering what we did well to make the ball fly how we wanted.

Tiger loved to play and compete in my weekly junior golf tournaments. When Tiger played with Earl and me, he played from the same tees as we did.

Because Tiger was much smaller in size we were getting a huge distance advantage. To balance this out I created 'Tiger Par' so the par of the hole was adjusted relative to how far he hit the ball at that point in time. This way he would know how he was playing relative to his personal par. He might get a six on what was a par-4 hole, but that was a Tiger Par because it took him four good shots to get on the green plus two putts.

As he began to hit the ball further the 'Tiger par' was adjusted accordingly. I remember one day we played together and he went out and shot eight under his personal par. He chose all his own shots, picked all of his own clubs and holed every putt.

He didn't hit the ball much further than 100 yards. He was just five years old – and not a big five-year-old at that.

But where you could really see his skill was around the green.

He could pitch, chip and putt like a tour pro.

I believe his short game was great because he had a natural ability to see the ball flight in advance and feel the club to make the ball fly the way he saw it.

It's much like driving a race car. Yes, to win a professional car race like the Indy 500 you need a fast car. But you also need to know how to drive a fast race car.

Even if I had an Indy 500 race car I would still never win the race because I don't know how to drive a race car.

The same is true in golf. You can have a great golf swing but if you don't know how to use it you will never win golf tournaments. No matter how great you hit the ball on the driving range. Using your swing to shoot low scores on the golf course is a completely different skill than that of hitting the ball on the driving range.

Since those days in the early 1980s with Tiger and Earl, my coaching has evolved from how I taught in the 1970s.

Now I spend very little time telling my students what to do, I just give them options to explore. Options that allow the player to develop their own game as opposed to trying to fit them into some kind of ideal swing model.

Today I call my coaching Guided Self Discovery.

It is all about the shots we play not the details of how the swing looks. A fade is not a bad shot. It may be inappropriate for this particular moment but if you can remember how it feels to play a fade then you have that shot available when you need it.

Building awareness of your own game is a vital skill to develop because you need to uncover your way to play.

We also need to have the freedom to explore by having a better relationship to poor outcomes. Learn to provide yourself an environment that allows exploration and a willingness to test out what happens with the ball when we apply the club in certain ways.

Learn from the bad and remember the good.

The concepts you are about to read in The Lost Art of Playing Golf resonate with my own philosophy about the 'art' of playing golf. Yes, science can be valuable but when you step out onto the golf course you need to have a game that is adaptable. A game that can produce the shot the golf course requires in each unique moment.

When you embrace the ideas Karl and Gary bring to The Lost Art of Playing Golf you have a chance to connect back to the very source of the game.

Of being like a kid and feeling the joy of creating a golf shot in your mind and then setting your body free to produce that shot.

That's what kids do in the playground and that's what I saw Tiger do when he was a kid on the golf course.

Gary and Karl bring this style of playing golf to life in this book. You will read, learn and then let your skill free to be as good as you can be. You will be able to use some of the ideas in the book to learn to play golf better and have more fun doing it. By following Gary and Karl's advice you will at the very least have a better relationship with the game that will allow you to get much closer to your true potential. **Enjoy your journey.**

About The Author

Rudy Duran has been a golf professional for over 48 years and is a respected coach and golf course owner/operator. He is best known for being Tiger Woods' first golf coach, from the age of four to 10. Currently, Rudy is working on his game, coaching and promoting golf worldwide.

Rudy turned professional in 1971 and has been a member of the PGA of America since 1976. He played on the PGA Tour in 1977 and 1978. He was inducted into the Long Beach California Golf Hall of Fame, received the PGA Tour's Card Walker Award for contributions to junior golf and was recognised as the Southern California PGA Northern Chapter Golf Professional of the Year three times.

AN
INTRODUCTION
from the authors

WHEN we set out to write our previous book, The Lost Art of Putting, the project was something of a labour of love. We just wanted to get our ideas down on paper. We had no idea of the reaction we were about to get. Pretty much since the book's launch at the 2018 Scottish Open we have been truly amazed at what has happened.

We have been No 1 on Amazon for many weeks and we get communication on a daily basis from golfers who have benefitted from the ideas in the book. It would seem that these ideas about 'The Lost Art' have captured a moment in golfing time.

We have access to more information than ever. As a golfer, you are inundated with prompts on YouTube, Twitter and the like to look at the latest must-do move or must-have gadget.

Yet what we know is all of this information is not making us better or happier golfers. If anything, the opposite.

It would seem the message we have given to people about reconnecting with your own creativity and the wisdom of your own body is really gathering pace. We hope the tide is turning. So many players have emailed us to say they have restored their love of putting as they are set free to create each and every individual putt in a unique moment in time.

We were hoping for this kind of response but we never expected it. We felt how you are on the greens was always going to be a reflection of how you are in the rest of the game so it seemed a logical next step that we put our heads together and got down on paper our collective ideas for the whole game.

We are tremendously excited to share with you here the next step in The Lost Art journey.

The Lost Art of Playing Golf drills down even deeper into the ideas of connecting with the very soul of the game and your ability as an individual to discover your way of doing things as opposed to us telling you our opinion on what we feel you should do.

As with The Lost Art of Putting, we are not saying you need to abandon technique and stop having lessons. We firmly believe that time spent with a trusted coach is one of the best investments you could possibly make for your game.

What we do have for you are some suggestions on how to take the game you have and deliver the results on the only stage that matters – the golf course.

We hope to engage your imagination on a journey of possibility.

Just imagine what it could feel like in the future if you have the ability to create unique golf shots in your mind and then have the trust and faith in your body to execute those intentions.

That singular ability to fall in love with the idea of creating golf shots is what most golfers have lost; to be comfortable on the golf course as a place you can explore and develop some of your true ability.

We will explore a number of concepts we feel will really resonate with you and get you to think about the whole game in a different way.

A way that will liberate you to enjoy more of your golfing days to come. As we will discuss in this book every single one of the golfing days you have left is a very precious entity in and of itself.

We want those remaining days to be filled with more fun, enjoyment, exploration and creativity.

We will at no point suggest results don't matter but what we will suggest to you is there may be a different route to those results than the one you are currently on.

The ideas and information you will read are not just our own whimsical musings – they are backed by the very latest research into how best to utilise the connection between mind and body.

We have enlisted the help of some of the world's leading experts in skill acquisition to support our case and we feel sure you will enjoy their ideas. If you have already read The Lost Art of Putting then we hope this book is a natural and exciting follow-on for you in your voyage of discovery.

If you are new to The Lost Art series then we welcome you aboard for what we hope will be the start of a new lease of your golfing life.

So let's get underway and dive straight in.

All the very best,
Gary and Karl

Key Takeaways

1 Golfers are inundated with information. This does not seem to be helpful. It is time we rediscovered the concept of creativity.

2 Imagine discovering, or rediscovering, the ability to create unique golf shots in your mind and then having the trust and faith in your body to execute those intentions.

3 This book will help you deal with whatever you may be feeling on the golf course, good or bad, and still get the task completed.

4 These aren't just our views – we are supported by some of the world's leading experts in skill acquisition.

Chapter 1
WHAT HAVE YOU GOT TO BE GRATEFUL ABOUT TODAY?

Your perception of the game of golf can fundamentally change for the better, explains Karl

Gratitude / ˈgratɪtjuːd / Noun. The quality of being thankful; readiness to show appreciation for and to return kindness.

MUCH of what we discuss in this book is about a shift in your attitude. A shift in the way the world occurs to you.

Instead of hoping that a bit more lag on the downswing is going to change your whole golfing experience, you get to change your experience from the inside out.

The irony is when you experience the game differently, when the way the game occurs to you changes, you then get to create the conditions that can allow better movements to emerge as a result of how your body is experiencing the game.

By the way you feel about the game and your experiences within that game. The inside can indeed change the outside.

However, without change on the inside then you will be locked into the long-term insanity of thinking the next swing position is going to be your golfing salvation.

I remember once being at a golf club in the south of England, a beautiful tree-lined course. It was a wonderful spring afternoon. The ground was beginning to dry out after a harsh and wet winter and the trees looked like they were ready to start flourishing for another year. It was easy to feel the sense of optimism spring brings with it each year.

As I walked the back nine I noticed a wooden bench next to a tee. There was a brass plaque with an inscription on the bench. Nothing unusual about this at a golf club, but the inscription in this particular instance was somewhat different.

It was a commemorative plaque that said: 'To The Tuesday Boys'.

Underneath the title were the names of four golfers and their years of birth and death. It seemed each of these four players had all passed away within a relatively close period of time. It was poignant to think of these four former golfers, no longer with us.

They had clearly played for many years together on a Tuesday – The Tuesday Boys.

I began to think of how many times they would have set out on a round of golf. How many times it would have been just another Tuesday. This ritual obviously went on week after week, year after year.

They would probably have got together on the 1st tee and said something about the state of their game, how they had been struggling with their tee shots, the week they had just had from the previous Tuesday and their hopes for the round ahead.

They must have gone through this routine time and time again. Played golf together on a Tuesday. They would have shared the highs and lows of the game. The emotions, both good and bad. The opportunity to sit in the clubhouse afterwards reflecting on the round and sharing in great conversation and friendship.

Then suddenly they had run out of Tuesdays. One by one, the Tuesday Boys must have got smaller in numbers as a group until they didn't have any Tuesdays left. The last putt had been holed and the opportunity to enjoy another round had gone forever.

This experience really reinforced to me the utter preciousness of each and every chance we have to play this wonderful game. The incredible way we all take for granted the fact that for us all there are unfortunately only a certain number of Tuesdays left.

None of us know how many Tuesdays it will be but don't we all labour under a certain illusion these opportunities will go on and on? There will always be another game to play. Another chance. Another Tuesday.

Richard Bandler, the co-founder of Neuro-linguistic Programming (NLP), said many years ago the greatest delusion human beings have is they think they are eternal. There will always be more opportunity in the future. Our future self is going to be better than our current self.

Well, at some point there won't be another opportunity. Every single one of us will at some point play our final round. We will sink a putt on the 18th green and it will be the last putt we ever hit.

The Skill Of Gratitude

Without being alarmist or a doom merchant, it is so important to embrace what for me is another vital key in the quest to unlock and reshape your golfing story and get the most out of this human experience. That is the skill of gratitude.

There is strong evidence to suggest that in the quest to feel good about ourselves and release our true capabilities the skill of gratitude is a huge asset.

For years, research has shown gratitude not only reduces stress but may also play a major role in overcoming trauma. A 2006 study published in Behaviour Research and Therapy found that Vietnam War Veterans with higher levels of gratitude experienced lower rates of Post-Traumatic Stress Disorder.

A 2003 study published in the Journal of Personality and Social Psychology found that gratitude was a major contributor to resilience following the terrorist attacks on September 11. Recognising all you have to be thankful for – even during the worst times of your life – fosters resilience.

When we embrace the feelings of gratitude we release into our systems a whole different bunch of chemicals. Our cortisol levels drop, stress reduces and our sense of wellbeing increases.

I have often said – we think if we play well we will feel good. But perhaps a different way to look at this is when we feel good we actually create the optimal conditions to play well.

We go first instead of waiting for the golf ball to make us feel good. If we are constantly waiting for the direction of a golf ball to make us feel good then we are condemning ourselves to spending a good deal of our life waiting. We will continue to walk an emotional tightrope.

It has become even more clear to me as a result of a personal family situation how easy it is to take experiences and people for granted. I watched my mother descend into the hell-hole that is dementia. I saw someone literally lose their mind. Lose the ability to walk. Lose the ability to talk.

Our mind is the most precious thing we own. Yet we take it so much for granted as life just flows by on a daily basis without us really paying attention and being awake.

The days, weeks and months pass by and the old cliche of you don't know what you have got until it is gone is very, very real.

Ask the question: What am I grateful for?

Just simply ask that question and meditate on the answer for a moment. What does it bring up? We really do forget it is often the very simplest things that, if we focus on them, make us feel incredibly good. Here and now today.

Yet the trick is to do this mindfully, to actually pay attention to what we are grateful for right now. Now, this book is not some hand-wringing encounter group designed to make you teary-eyed. It is a book all about performance. But, as you are hopefully understanding, the way you actually create the conditions for performance is often paradoxical in nature. Feel good to play good. Who would imagine that? So, in the quest to change your golfing story, how would it be if you embraced the power of gratitude?

As we always say, the key to this information is to personalise it. But, as a suggestion, how do you think it would be if, before you play golf, you just asked the question: 'What am I grateful for today?'

Maybe just think for a moment before you get out of the car. Just pause for a split second before you go rushing off to the 1st tee on auto-pilot. Just ask the question 'what am I grateful for today' and then ponder on the answer.

What do you think might emerge as a result of this simple ritual?

The reports from many players over the past few years have been nothing short of transformational in terms of their story.

By asking and answering this particular question a lot of their previous anxiety about trying to perform just tends to drift away.

So much anxiety is created by projecting far ahead into an imaginary future that hasn't happened yet.

We are playing this for that – in the sense we are playing this round of golf for what we perceive it may bring us at some point in the future.

Be that anything from lowering our handicap to winning a major.

Yet to be grateful here and now today for the opportunity to play grounds us in the here and now.

The paradox is the more grateful we are to take the opportunity to play today, the more we create the conditions of being in the place all of the sports psychology books tell us to be: The present moment.

By being a little bit more grateful to be here, we then tend to focus on the here and now. We become absorbed in this round here and now for its own sake as opposed to being carried off into the future land of make believe. At the very least by embracing gratitude we get to feel good right away. The key is to set this as a clear frame of mind before you begin your round.

Once you begin to play and some of the chaos that is golf begins, it is tough to connect with the sense of being grateful as we get drawn into the story of outcome and what we think should be happening. The pre-round commitment is a way to get the best out of your day regardless of the final number on the scorecard.

Gratitude reduces a multitude of toxic emotions, ranging from envy and resentment to frustration and regret.

Robert A. Emmons, Ph.D., a leading gratitude researcher, has conducted multiple studies on the link between gratitude and wellbeing. His research confirms that gratitude effectively increases happiness and reduces depression.

The experience many players report back with is they tend to appreciate the golf course. They appreciate the work that has been done to give us this opportunity.

It can all seem a little trite but I can tell you, with as much certainty as I have, the concept of gratitude is a very powerful weapon in the quest to change your story.

One of the caveats to this concept, though, is to be aware of what I call false gratitude, or gratitude with strings attached. This is when you pretend to be grateful thinking that if you are grateful then you will play well. It doesn't work that way.

This is a big trap to fall into and the opposite of what we are suggesting here. It is about being grateful for this opportunity to play. The opportunity to walk around a golf course, in nature with the company of others. The opportunity to move your body, to test yourself and see what you can achieve.

The outcome will be what it will be but you are providing the conditions to allow a good performance to emerge.

It is interesting to consider before you go out to play just what a tiny percentage of the people in the world have this kind of opportunity. And to consider all of the work that will have gone on before you step onto the course. The greens staff who will have been there at the crack of dawn preparing the greens and fairways so that you have the chance to play.

The irony is that if you are grateful you become more open to your surroundings, and in doing so you actually take in more of the information the golf course is giving you.

You start to see with a clearer lens just what the course designer is doing with the way the holes are laid out. You can then create the shots appropriate to the challenge you now see.

Key Takeaways

1 The Tuesday Boys ran out of Tuesdays. The same will happen to us all one day. Don't take your golf for granted. Opportunities to play are not limitless.

2 Recognising all you have to be thankful for – even during the worst times of your life – fosters resilience and creates the optimal conditions to play well.

3 Before you get out of your car at the golf club, take a moment to ask yourself: What am I grateful for today?

4 Be aware of false gratitude. If you pretend to be grateful so you will then play well, then you will be disappointed. It doesn't work that way. It is about being grateful for whatever shows up today.

Chapter 2
WHAT'S THE MOST IMPORTANT QUESTION A GOLFER CAN ASK?

Think back to why you started playing. How do those feelings compare to your current golfing experiences?

Question / ˈkwɛstʃ(ə)n / Noun. A sentence worded or expressed so as to elicit information.

YOU will hear throughout this book the importance and value of effective questions. Now is the time to ask you to consider as you read this book: What is the most important question a golfer can ever ask?

Maybe ponder that for just a moment before your eyes skip down to the next paragraph because we really do feel it is that important.

We do not think it is 'how do I cure my slice?' or 'how can I get a few more yards of the tee?' but simply: 'Why do I play golf?'

Such a simple question, such a short question, but unless you are brutally honest with yourself about the answer we believe your progress will always be somewhat limited.

If you have a big enough why then you will always find the how. So why do you play golf?

Be careful as your brain creates an answer for you because it is likely the answer is a conditioned response to what you think you should say – even to yourself. Our premise is that since you began to play the game in the first place, the reasons you kept striving to get better may well have been hijacked, for reasons we will explain.

The culture of the game and the messages from certain sections of media may well have skewed your thinking.

What we want to stress more than anything is that we believe for you to get the most from your remaining time with the game of golf you need to be playing for your own reasons.

Not anyone else's construction of the purpose of the game.

The authentic reasons for you as an individual. When you are in touch with your truth then you can begin to play a game really worth all of the time and effort.

Many players we have worked with over the years have been liberated when they actually give themselves permission to play 'their' game as opposed to 'the' game.

One way you can begin to unlock the answer to the question is to go back to the beginning. Just take some time to think back to the very earliest memories you have of the game.

How did it all start for you? What was it about this strange ball and stick game that drew you in the first place? How did the relationship begin? Who got you started?

Cast your mind back to what may for some be a very distant past and allow the vault of your mind to open up to the memories of where it all began. The reason for this is your first attempts to play the game were more than likely taken for the purest of reasons.

Something in the game itself captured your imagination and got you interested, the game drew you in. At the very earliest stages, it probably wasn't about what golf could bring you in the future it was about what golf provided you in the present.

For many, the sheer joy of swinging a club through space and finally making good contact with the ball and seeing it fly up into the sky started a love affair that lasted a lifetime.

If you took up the game as a junior, you probably spent countless summer days and nights out on the course playing hole after hole.

Why Karl Started Playing Golf

When I was still at school I used to sit in lessons and instead of paying attention to the teacher I began to think about shots hit on the golf course. I couldn't wait for the next opportunity to get out and just play the game. No wonder I did so poorly at school.

The summer holidays were often filled with anything up to 54 holes of golf in a single day.

You couldn't wait for the sun to come up so you could get to the golf course. You played one round and then lunch was something of an inconvenient necessity getting in the way of playing more golf.

At the golf course I used to play as a junior, Leigh, the 12th is a lovely par 3. It's only short but guarded by a stream and surrounded by bunkers. The main road beside the green is out of bounds. The best part of it as a junior was the fact that by the side of the green was a street lamp. This provided us juniors with perfect late-night illumination as we played chipping games as night descended. This lamp allowed us to squeeze just a few more shots out of the day that we wanted to hang on to for as long as possible.

None of this ever seemed like it was 'working' at the game. It was just sheer fun and enjoyment as we were lost in creating all kinds of shots around that 12th green until it was literally pitch dark. There was nothing better than seeing a bunker shot fizz to a halt a couple of feet from the flag as the sticky heat of the summer's day turned into that particular kind of beautiful late-evening experience when the wind often dies down and you are immersed in your experience.

Yes, we were breaking the 'no chipping' rules of the club but it was a pure and wonderful opportunity to be playing the game just for the sheer joy it gave to us. Of course at the time we didn't know that. We were just kids playing a game but it is only now we can look through the strained lens of adult eyes we can understand just what a pure experience it was. It was golf for its own sake. Playing the game for the sake of the game.

Then something changed. As I got better at golf and started to be told I had 'potential' my relationship with the game began to change.

Sure, I enjoyed the attention as I got 'better', and the words bolstered my ego but looking back it was a dangerous game I had begun to play.

Slowly but surely golf became about what it was going to help me become in the future as opposed to what I was experiencing in the now. The lines began to blur.

Golf went from something that I did to something that I was. If I shot 70 I was a good person yet if I shot 80 I felt worthless.

When golf goes from something that you do to something that you are then the stakes become very high. Your identity is on the line every time you tee up the ball. That's not a good place to be.

Every practice session wasn't about skill or mastery of creating golf shots it was a means to hopefully provide the end of more adulation and attention. Practice became a desperate attempt to 'hold on' to my swing and hope it wouldn't let me down in a tournament.

Years later, when my relationship with the game had deteriorated completely, I read an article commenting on Tiger Woods's upbringing. Chuck Hogan, a pioneering coach, talked about how Earl Woods had provided the young Tiger with a 'safe place' to play the game. He made it very clear to the young genius: if he had a bad day on the course then it was Tiger Woods the golfer and not Tiger Woods the person. This allowed Woods to play the game.

We are not in any way saying here competition is bad or striving to be the best you can be or getting your handicap cut is a bad thing. Far from it. But what we are saying is that if you are not clear as to why you are playing the game then you can very easily fall into an ego-induced trap that is very difficult to escape from.

If golf has the ability to make you a somebody then it also has the ability to make you a nobody. Yes, the game is precious, but to give it such authority over you is wrong.

What Makes You Happy About Golf?

To strive to be the very best you can possibly be, we think, is a great reason to play the game. But the line shouldn't blur so golf becomes something you are as opposed to something you do.

To embark on a journey of personal mastery would be a wonderful answer to the fundamental question of why you play.

As the legendary golf coach Fred Shoemaker said: "To fall in love with the idea of mastering a game you will never master.""

This is a perspective about what you can do to improve yourself as opposed to falling into the ego trap of comparison with others.

We do however know how difficult this can be in a world consumed with comparison but if you get really clear on your reasons to play you can steer yourself through the choppy waters and come out the other side.

When you are really clear as to why you play the game then it is much easier to stay with that commitment when you do actually play. If you decide the social interaction of the game is very important to you then make sure you honour that commitment when you play.

This doesn't have to be at the expense of good scoring. We know far too many club players who are very social in practice games and then they withdraw into their self-imposed shell when a competition is being played and then wonder why they can't take their practice game into competition.

To play well at golf is to be in balance in more than just your golf swing. We are a dynamic human organism interacting with a dynamic environment and it is important to see the whole and not just the isolated part that is the top of your backswing.

Maybe it is being outdoors that is really important to you. The research is very clear from numerous sources: being outside in nature is extremely good for our mental wellbeing.

If this is one of your key reasons to play golf then, again, make sure when you play that you actually honour that reason. We discussed in Chapter 1 the importance of gratitude – suffice to say the opportunity for you to be out on the golf course, close to nature, in a wonderful environment is a very precious opportunity.

If being competitive is the fuel firing your flames, that is tremendous. See the opportunity to be stretched, to be tested. You can then see the good play of others not as a threat but as a trigger to drive you to greater things.

Think about the way that Henrik Stenson and Phil Mickelson in the 2016 Open Championship at Troon drew out of each other golf of an unbelievable quality as they traded blow for wonderful blow on that magnificent Sunday afternoon.

Stress is a word which gets a bad reputation in the modern world but just like a muscle needs to be given a load to bear to keep strong a certain amount of stress is good for our mind as well if we deal with it in the right way.

Understand that being competitive will bring with it some feelings of discomfort. You may well feel uneasy on the 1st tee as a result of your competitive drive.

What we do know is that if your attention is on the right elements of the game, as we will show you, then you can still perform even in the presence of some discomfort. Rather than trying to make all the discomfort go away, be clear, because you are competitive that is part of the deal.

The message to yourself should be you can perform well with those feelings if you have the skills of effective attention. So it is a case of 'I have these feelings of discomfort and I can perform' as opposed to wanting to banish or block feelings and emotions.

The paradox is when we embrace the feelings of discomfort they actually lose their power. Whatever we resist, we strengthen – so when we try to avoid or push away uncomfortable feelings they only tighten their grip over us.

Hopefully, you can begin to see the absolute necessity of being really clear as to why you are actually playing the game of golf.

It's the need to uphold your truth as opposed to anyone else's.

Be true to your own reasons for engaging in golf and then you provide a foundation for all of the other tools and techniques you will learn in the rest of this book.

When you are clear with your why you then stand a very good chance of finding the how.

Take Responsibility For Your Golf

I think we would all agree that the game of golf is very much a window to the soul.

Whatever we have inside of us the game of golf will tend to reveal. Consider when you get to play the game with a stranger. We shake hands on the 1st tee and exchange all of the usual pleasantries: Play well, have a good game, good luck. We have all uttered these phrases many times. You begin the round of golf and during the next four hours the stranger you shook hands with on the 1st tee starts to reveal their personality to you and of course you to them.

You get to see so much. The truth is revealed bit by bit, hole by hole. How someone deals with adversity, how they cope with unexpected success, the warmth of their personality, their generosity of spirit or lack thereof, their ability to ride the storms of chaos the game of golf inevitably throws at us.

By the conclusion of 18 holes you usually have a sense the person you have just shared the experience with is the kind of person to either give you energy or the type to drain that energy.

As much as many players would like to blame anything other than themselves, in the end the game of golf always points the finger of responsibility back at you.

It would seem in this current day and age taking responsibility is seen as something from a bygone age. We tend to want to attribute the way we feel to other people and to circumstances. If we can lay the blame at the feet of others we often take that choice.

The crazy world of social media is awash with a culture of blame and retribution: a strong sense of wanting to take offence, of hair-trigger responses when confronted with a different viewpoint.

Yet what does this bring us in the long run – happiness and a sense of satisfaction?

It would seem not. To take responsibility of your place in the world is to take on a monumental burden. The load is heavy. It is far from easy.

Yet when we do decide to take genuine responsibility for our actions and our deeds we put ourselves in a position that can foster genuine satisfaction.

Yes, this is a golf book and we may seem to be heading into some deep waters here, but these are the kind of questions we feel are more important than if you are on or off plane. When you genuinely decide to take responsibility you actually create the conditions to liberate yourself from the tyranny of blame and entitlement.

You are suddenly set free from the shackles of wanting others or the world to behave in a certain way to suit your own perceptions.

You can take responsibility for your golf game. You can take the decision that you want to actually develop some skills that will be hard to master but in the long run can give you endless pleasure.

You can take responsibility for your experience of the game regardless of what the golf ball may or may not be doing on any singular occasion.

To take responsibility for your reactions to what the golf ball does is again to bear a heavy load.

Yet what is the alternative – to react like a spoilt child because the golf ball is not doing what you think it should? It is much, much easier to abstain from taking responsibility than it is to embrace it.

Yet just imagine if the game of golf provided you with a huge laboratory full of equipment designed to test you in ways that shape the whole of your life.

If you can take responsibility for the way you experience the game of golf and the way the game occurs to you then you can explore taking responsibility for the whole shooting match of your life.

What would it be like to be just that bit better at dealing with what the world and others threw at you? To never again feel entitled to expect someone else to behave in a certain way or to be entitled for the world to provide you with certain circumstances.

To develop resilience is a wonderful golfing skill but far more importantly it is a phenomenal life skill that builds in you a genuine sense of being able to go forwards towards your goals and deal with whatever chaos is thrown at you.

It is very easy to look at a generation of people and say they are soft and can't deal with life. Yet they are only executing the attitudes handed to them by the previous generation. To expect anything in life is to play a very dangerous game. To expect anything in golf is to put yourself on the path to continual disappointment and at times abject misery.

We have developed a mantra with many tour players over the years along the lines of: 'Expect nothing, deal with everything.'

Just consider that idea for a moment.

It has been around long enough to be a cliche but the phrase ' the man with no expectation will never be disappointed' has some strong strands of wisdom encased in apparent platitude.

When you let go of expectation and you embrace the idea of dealing with anything thrown at you then you actually set yourself free to immerse yourself in this round, this shot.

You get to create golf shots with clear intent knowing you will take the responsibility for whatever the outcome is.

The ancient stoics talked about the 'circle of control' and how a life well lived involved being extremely clear what was and what wasn't in your circle of control.

When we examine this premise, the sledgehammer of truth is that the only aspect within our circle of control is our mind, our responses and decisions. Other people are not in that circle as much as we would sometimes like them to be. The events of the outside world are not in that circle. The list goes on and on.

Not even our own body is in that circle. We can get sick for reasons beyond our control. The harrowing truth and the great liberation is that our mind and its responses do lie within this circle.

Yes, we embrace a mighty responsibility to embrace this principle but the moment we do, the locks and chains are removed and we get the chance to embrace our life and our truth in the way we best see fit.

The Reaction Challenge

So much emphasis in golf is on what you do before you hit the shot and even more emphasis is on the shot itself. Yet we have found a great way to improve your game is to look at and take responsibility for what happens after the ball has left the club.

When golf is analysed on TV the format has remained the same for as long as high-speed video has been available. The names of the players may change and the experts will be different but the same system will apply.

The player hits a poor shot and the expert gets to view their swing and they know the ball has gone to the left or to the right.

The analysis takes place and we are told the player 'flipped his hands' or 'he got trapped on the inside'.

It all sounds wonderful and the expert puffs out his chest as he bestows his wisdom on a grateful audience of lesser golfing beings. Yet how can this be the whole truth? That same player didn't seem to be being trapped on whatever the inside is for the previous 13 holes. How inconvenient that the inside just suddenly reared its ugly head at that moment.

Yet if we were perhaps brave enough to look a little deeper and we go back to the previous green and we see the very same player three putt from 15 feet after hitting two great shots into a par 4. And we then see that same player explode at his caddie as he walks off the green for giving him a bad read. And as we see the same player pull out his driver on the next tee still trying to digest what has just happened. Do you think the rush of emotion he is feeling and the anger rattling his particular cage might have some possible impact on the shot the 'expert' has so forthrightly described?

Of course it has to have had an impact.

The said player was dealing with a flood of chemicals rushing through his system and expecting to make a good swing.

It wasn't because he suddenly found 'the inside' it was more to do with the fact that he didn't own his reaction to the previous shot.

His reaction to the previous shot contaminated his ability to create the shot in front of him. The shot then sails off line.

We ignore the way we react to golf shots to the detriment of a great potential breakthrough. This strategy can have an instant impact the very next time you play basically by taking a decision to take responsibility for your reactions. To react in a way that is not just an auto-pilot response to a sense of entitlement that the game should be giving you more than it actually is.

How many poor shots do you think you have hit in the past are a result of the residue of a previous shot?

How many times do you think you have gone on a run of bad holes as a result of the fact you didn't take responsibility for the way you reacted to where a golf ball flew?

This is the really exciting part.

The opportunity that comes with making the decision to take responsibility. To totally own your reactions and your responses.

Your ability to create great golf shots has the potential to soar if you are prepared to engage with this.

If you are prepared to deal with whatever the golf ball does then you are actually free to create the shots you truly desire.

Key Takeaways

1 If you have a big enough why then you will always find the how. So why do you play golf?

2 Most of us start playing golf for the purest of reasons – like the sheer joy of swinging a club and making good contact with the ball. Can you remember these feelings?

3 One wonderful answer to the fundamental question of why you play is: To embark on a journey of personal mastery.

4 Be really clear as to why you actually play the game of golf. Make sure you are upholding your truth as opposed to anyone else's.

5 By taking genuine responsibility for our golf we put ourselves in a position that can foster genuine satisfaction.

STUDYING ARCHITECTURE MAKES YOU A BETTER GOLFER

Mike Clayton on how understanding the principles of architecture can hugely increase your enjoyment of the game

I N the space of two weeks in late 1989, Australia's Peter Fowler won both the team event (with Wayne Grady) and the individual title at the World Cup in Spain and then, after an arduous flight home, he came third in the Australian Open at Kingston Heath.

The great Peter Thomson was leading the television commentary and in the car park after the final round the pair ran into each other. Thomson congratulated Fowler on his fine play and Fowler asked the five-time Open champion what he could do to improve his golf.

"Shoot lower scores, Peter," said Thomson. "Shoot lower scores."

Fowler would later tell me: "For years I was upset with him and what seemed to be such a flippant response but that was my problem for completely misunderstanding what he was telling me.

"He was saying to me, stop stressing so much about your swing and focus on the point of the game," said Fowler.

The game and its golf courses are inextricably linked and in no other game are the fields of play so important and so diverse.

Whoever heard of flying across the world to experience a tennis court, a football pitch or a high jump pit?

The point of a golf course is to encourage good play, to ask enduringly interesting questions testing both thought and execution and to inspire players to learn new shots while still giving poorer players a way around. These four critical points are at the heart of almost every great course.

There are always exceptions, though, and the one thing we must not do is assume golf course design is founded on hard and fast rules because for every accepted principle there is a great course or a great hole sure to break it.

Merion, for example, has only two par 5s, the second of which you have played by the time you stand on the 5th tee.

Can anyone imagine making the Alps Hole at Prestwick, the 13th hole at North Berwick, the Road Hole or the blind tee shot off Sunningdale's 7th and avoid the wrath and the criticism from those who think golf should be 'fair'?

These great holes prove patently it isn't, never was and should never be. Dealing with the inherent unfairness of the game is its great mental challenge.

Once at an Open Championship a journalist sympathised with an unfair bounce that Jack Nicklaus had endured. "Of course it wasn't fair," said Nicklaus. "But the game wasn't supposed to be fair."

Pine Valley, unquestionably one of golf's greatest playgrounds, encourages good play, tests thought and execution and encourages the acquisition of new shots that 'players have hitherto been unable to play', as Alister MacKenzie put it. However, Pine Valley absolutely doesn't give poor players a way around the trouble. If you can't hit it and you care about the card and pencil in your back pocket you're bound to have a brutal day at Pine Valley.

The mistake of many good players, as well the arrangers of courses used on the world's professional tours, is thinking a course should purely be a test of execution. It's hardly surprising. If you're a pro you want the best hitter to win and you want the course to be 'fair' and 'right there in front of you'. Ugh.

The problem arises when people equate straight hitting with good play and their only way to define, to examine, good driving is to play down narrow holes lined with penal rough and, by definition, devoid of any interesting questions because the only answer to the question is to hit straight.

You don't have to think where you might want to play because the architect or the course set-up guy is already dictating where to aim and what club to hit. This is not the lesson of the Old Course at St Andrews, the great architect Alister MacKenzie's favourite course and Thomson's ideal model.

MacKenzie was once asked to compare the Old Course with Cypress Point, unquestionably the most beautiful course he designed.

"St Andrews cannot be compared with Cypress Point," he said. "St Andrews is first class, there is no second and Cypress Point comes in a very bad third."

It's the best course in the world and in an extraordinary run of holes coming in from the far end of the course it boasts one of the best short par 4s (the 12th), one of the best mid-length two shotters (the 16th), two of the best long 4s (the 13th and 17th) and the greatest par 5 in the game (the 14th).

These holes ask the most nuanced of questions, offer a wide variety of alternate lines and shots and have proved to be the most enduringly interesting holes in the game. And mostly they can be played with a putter – one of Thomson's definitions of a worthwhile hole. St Andrews is wide enough to give players enough space from the tee to swing with freedom and this was one lesson MacKenzie took from the Old Course.

In his seminal book, The Spirit of St Andrews, he argued: "Narrow fairways bordered by long grass make bad golfers. They do so by destroying the harmony and continuity of the game and in causing a stilted and a cramped style, destroying all freedom of play."

Mackenzie well understood the importance of good and interesting course design to the future progress and popularity of the game. Good courses weren't out to punish the poorest shots of the worst players but rather to draw out and inspire great golf from good players.

Lest you think he was only concerned with good players, his courses prove otherwise as he was a brilliant designer of courses to be enjoyed by all standards of players.

He suggested the reason people gave up golf was because the courses they were playing were not 'real courses'.

"There may be no interest or strategy about it; it simply gives him an opportunity for exercise and 'socking' a golf ball," he wrote. "He is opposed to any alterations being made to it, but the time inevitably comes when he gets tired of golf, without knowing the reason why."

A contemporary of MacKenzie, the American Max Behr articulated something similar when he wrote: "The object of golf architecture is to give an intelligent purpose to the striking of a golf ball. To be worthwhile, this purpose must excite and hold interest. If it fails in this, the character of the architecture is at fault."

These men were working and writing in the 1920s and 1930s but when it comes to the principles of good golf course design nothing has changed since.

The best modern-day architects are emulating the principles and in many cases the look of the best courses of the Golden Era of course design. Sadly they are also in a seemingly never-ending chase to keep up with manufacturers of balls and clubs bent on making so many of the greatest courses obsolete for the best players in the game. At some point we all run out of land.

For good players, a fertile imagination or a love of great golf course design aren't things likely to be of much help on the professional tour. Professional golf is all about money and the quality of the golf course architecture is far down the list of priorities of players, sponsors, television and the tour.

If you're a good player and you want to compete on great courses find a nice job and play amateur golf.

Either way, even the dullest of holes ask questions. They're just not particularly interesting questions but if they ask for two classy, long shots golf pros will likely approve and even praise the hole and the course, especially if they are presented in perfect condition.

The architect hasn't contributed anything to put confusion or doubt but nor has he made anything to inspire or draw from a player a truly great shot.

Severiano Ballesteros at his best played with more inspiration than anyone before or since (OK – I'll give you Tiger Woods) and he rarely played with confusion or doubt. Not until the dark days at the end of his career anyway.

There is a connection with Ballesteros, great design and Alister MacKenzie. He is the only man to have won big championships at MacKenzie's favourite, the Old Course, and the finest courses professional golf visits with any regularity at Augusta and Royal Melbourne.

Because MacKenzie so understood St Andrews he was able to translate the principles on to quite different sites, one on sand a mile from the sea in Melbourne and the other over hilly, red clay in Georgia. He gave Ballesteros – and Tiger Woods, Arnold Palmer and Jack Nicklaus – space to play from the tee and if they drove to their disadvantage he gave them a chance to play the great recovery but at the risk of playing their way into even more trouble.

As Bobby Jones once said he was "giving a man just enough rope to hang himself".

Unsurprisingly, Woods and Nicklaus both mastered the Old Course, each winning two Opens each there and Palmer, on his first foray to the Open in 1960, was only a shot behind the great Australian, Kel Nagle.

This is one element to the making of a great course. Anyone can hack out of long, thick, green grass (think of a typical US Open or the Ryder Cup in Paris) and make a bogey but the chance to make a par (or even a birdie) from the bad place but with a good lie is what leads to the bigger numbers or the truly heroic shots.

Phil Mickelson's 6-iron from behind the pine tree and off the pine needles at Augusta's 13th is an obvious example.

This is where the mental side of the game comes to the fore. Can you get inside the head of the architect and determine the question he is asking?

Can you pick the right shot when the right shot might vary from day to day and week to week depending on how you feel, the wind, the state of a tournament or even the position of the pin?

Tiger Woods masterful performance over the final nine holes at Augusta in 2019 showed off a truly great player not only in control of his game but a player understanding exactly the questions MacKenzie (and Robert Trent-Jones who revised MacKenzie's 16th hole) was asking and how to answer them by taking chances but not chances likely to cost him the tournament.

How could four of the very best players in the world – Tony Finau, Brooks Koepka, Ian Poulter and Francesco Molinari – all dump 145-yard shots into the creek fronting the 12th green while Woods played safely far to the left of the pin with an 8-iron?

"Shoot lower scores, Peter, shoot lower scores," said Thomson.

'It's a good course because I hit every club in the bag' – we so often hear this cliche wheeled out in praise a course when in reality there isn't any material difference between a 2, 3 or 4-iron or a 5 and a 6 or an 8,9 or 45-degree 'wedge'.

(And Tiger Woods pretty much played the final day at Augusta with a driver and an 8-iron – but at least that was an improvement on 1997 when it was primarily driver and wedge.)

What is more interesting and what you are much less likely to hear is: 'The course asked me to make so many interesting and perplexing choices and it asked me to hit every shot in the game.'

Of course, not many players can play every shot in the game (Sam Snead, another to win at St Andrews and Augusta, likely came the closest) so by definition we are all compromising in some way but there are basic elements of shotmaking the architect should legitimately employ to determine the skill and imagination of a player.

The classic Biarritz green (high sections in the front and back separated by a deep swale in the middle) was employed most often by CB Macdonald and Seth Raynor to test a player's ability to play a low, running shot landing short of the swale and running up through it to get to the back pin. Or to hit a high, spinning shot to stop on the front level if the pin was cut short.

The great Redan at North Berwick (15th) is one of the most copied holes in golf and it tests a player's ability to land a right-to-left tee shot in the front-right quarter of the green and feed the ball down to a back-left pin. Or to play the high, stopping shot over the longer diagonal carry across the guarding front-left bunker. Macdonald and Raynor made a masterful copies all over the United States including the 4th hole at the National Golf Links of America and Chicago Golf Club's dramatic, almost freakish, 7th.

MacKenzie, at his delightfully tempting 300-yard, par-4 10th at Royal Melbourne, made a tee shot quite easily played safely right with a long iron but every yard further right of the fearsome fairway bunker cut into the dune, a yard longer the pitch becomes. The pitch – anywhere from 30 yards to 90 or 100 – is protected in the front by a swale sweeping up anything remotely feeble and off the back is a steep slope taking a shot a yard long 40 fearsome yards away from the green. It becomes a real test of nerve to pitch all the way back to the back flag and only after pitching 20 feet short do you admonish yourself for not being braver.

In Ballesteros's first go at Royal Melbourne in 1978 he eschewed caution, instead flying his driver at the distant green each day. No one – not even Greg Norman – in the days of persimmon and balata tried it back then but Ballesteros was so sure of his recovery play he drove perfectly (you could have put a blanket over all four tee shots) into the sandy, heathy scrub five or ten paces short of the green and then blasted beautiful little sand wedges out to a few feet.

Three birdies was his reward for the week and while MacKenzie never knew Ballesteros he was an admirer of the great Walter Hagen. Hagen played with all the flair of Ballesteros and it was for men like Ballesteros and Woods that MacKenzie was designing golf courses. They were the ones he was trying to encourage because he knew interesting golf played with flair was the way to popularise the game.

George Thomas, the master American architect who made both Riviera and Los Angeles Country Club, wrote: "The strategy of the golf course is the soul of the game.

"The spirit of golf is to dare a hazard, and by negotiating it reap a reward while he who fears or declines the issue of the carry has a longer of harder shot for his second; yet the player who avoids the unwise effort gains advantage over one who tries for more than in him lies, or who fails under the test."

There is no point to width – a critical element of strategy – if it is not used wisely. The ideal line on to the flag is ideally protected by hazard and the irony of strategic golf is it usually relies on penal hazards for the strategy. At Carnoustie's 6th, it's the most penal hazard, an out of bounds fence. Likewise the 17th at St Andrews or the opener at Prestwick.

Royal Melbourne's long, par-4 17th is an example of perfect design as is the 13th at Augusta. At both holes MacKenzie made the test a fairway rewarding (more so at Augusta than Royal Melbourne) a right-to-left tee shot with a penal hazard on the inside guarding the boldest line. Then he built greens built on a diagonal and guarded by a hazard (a creek at Augusta and deep sand at Royal Melbourne) short and right to favour a left-to-right approach.

You can play both with a left-to-right tee shot (aiming at the trouble and playing away) and a right-to-left approach (playing at the trouble and moving away) but it's not the ideal and woe betide the straight shot and the first rule of golf – of shooting lower scores –never to hit a straight shot at and into trouble.

What these great and wide holes show off are quite different shots from one side of the fairway to the other.

Never was this better exemplified than in the classic duel between Ballesteros and Tom Watson at St Andews in the 1984 Open Championship. At the 71st hole Ballesteros drove safely away left into the rough, mindful perhaps of blowing his chance in the 1978 Open when, on the second day and playing beautiful golf, he blew a drive into the hotel and made seven.

From the poorest of angles he was asked to hit the great shot from a flier lie to find the green. Taking it on and messing up meant risking a six and surely losing the championship. Watson, in the group behind, drove bravely down the right and close to the boundary and from the perfect angle he chose either the wrong club or the wrong shot (or both) and made the bogey which ultimately cost him a chance at his sixth Open.

In theory, Ballesteros should have made the bogey and Watson the par but here was an example of a great hole – maybe the best hole in the game – testing the drive (a test won by the American) but then choices, nerve and skill in equal measure.

Ballesteros made the right choices and Watson the wrong ones but it's hard to imagine two players confronted by two such wildly different second shots on the same hole. Not many courses can look like St Andrews but they can adopt the principles and the questions making it the most enduringly popular course in the game.

It has its detractors, its critics, but it's a fair bet they don't understand the course and what it's asking. It's the most complicated and nuanced course in the game and if you can meet its challenges you are well on the way to understanding how to get around any course and shooting lower scores.

About The Author

Mike Clayton started as a caddy and played his way through junior and amateur golf, winning the Victorian Amateur twice and the Australian Amateur in 1978. He turned pro at the end of 1981, won the Victorian Open in early 1982 and headed to Europe where he played until 1996, winning the 1984 Timex Open.

Along with John Sloan and Bruce Grant, he started a golf design business in 1995. Their first client was Victoria Golf Club, the home course of Peter Thomson and then 18-year-old Geoff Ogilvy – who is now a partner in the architectural partnership of Ogilvy, Clayton, Cocking and Mead.

They all grew up playing on the Melbourne Sandbelt and the quality of those courses, including Royal Melbourne and Kingston Heath, aroused a passion for great golf course design. They have worked on many of Australia's best courses including Kingston Heath, Lake Karrinyup, The Lakes and Royal Queensland, as well as co-designing Tasmania's Barnbougle Dunes with Tom Doak.

Chapter 3
DOES THE SWING CREATE THE SHOT OR DOES THE SHOT CREATE THE SWING?

Are you focussing on form at the expense of function?

Create / kriːeɪt / Verb. To cause to come into being, as something unique that would not normally evolve or that is not made by ordinary process.

HISTORICALLY we have all been told and led to believe that if we make a good swing, we'll hit a good shot. Sound familiar? The golf coaching industry and the culture it has created has led us all down that path for decades, largely without foundation or success.

Our belief is this concept is fundamentally flawed.

Over the years we have seen far too many extremely talented players lose their way and ultimately their game as a direct result of their pursuit of the perfect swing, whatever that looks like.

Rather than asking 'what is wrong with my golf swing?' would it not make more sense to ask 'what is wrong with my shots?'

Trying to figure out what is wrong with your swing will have you questioning 101 different 'moves' and there will be no shortage of opinions on what you are doing wrong, most of which will be clichés at best and simply incorrect at worst.

By contrast, if you reflect on what happened with your shot, you will come up with facts, not opinions. If your tee shot finished in the left rough, or your approach shot finished short and right of the green, these are facts and not opinions.

The journeys from the left rough back to the fairway or the front right bunker to the green are a whole lot shorter and easier to correct and improve upon than the eternal, fruitless search for technical perfection. The golf course demands you create shots, not make pretty golf swings.

As you will have gleaned by now, our desire is to help you find your way of playing better golf and having more fun, rather than the way. Think about some of the most exciting and entertaining players over the years. Seve, of course, Phil Mickelson, Bubba Watson, Lee Trevino, Tom Watson and the King, Arnold Palmer, to name but a few. All great to watch. All artists who had us on the edge of our seats at one time or another. All golfers who found their way of playing this great game.

Palmer famously said: "Swing your swing. Not some idea of a swing. Not a swing you saw on TV. Not that swing you wish you had. No, swing your swing. Capable of greatness. Prized only by you. Perfect in its imperfection. Swing your swing. I know I did."

Tiger Woods would obviously be high up on anyone's list of creative golfers. The greatest player of the modern era once said: "My greatest strength is my creative mind."

In the run-up to the Open Championship at Carnoustie in 2018, Tiger talked about how the conditions would play a major role in how he was going to plot his way around the famous Scottish links.

With Scotland experiencing a lengthy heatwave – yes it does happen once in a blue moon – Carnoustie was burnt yellow and running harder and faster than it had done for decades.

Tiger said: "At Carnoustie there are not many opportunities to hit driver because the ball is going to roll 80 yards, so it's hard to keep the ball in play.

"I hit a 3-iron 333 yards in practice on the 18th hole, so when I get a bit older I can still chase a long club down there. Distance becomes a moot point but creativity plays such an important role. There's a reason Tom Watson won five Open Championships – he was very creative."

Tiger talked about his first taste of links golf when he played in the 1995 Scottish Open at Carnoustie as a 19-year-old amateur and recalled playing the par-4 2nd hole and "being close to 120 yards out and putting it. I'd never done that before – that was one of the cooler moments. I spent two hours on the driving range hitting the ball to the 100-yard sign. I was hitting 9-iron, 4-iron, 5-iron, just having a blast trying to hit the sign, being creative and using my mind."

Tiger finished tied T7th in the 1999 Open, 12th in 2007 and T6th in 2018. While he has never won (yet) at Carnoustie, it would be fair to say he found his way round the grand old links through using his imagination, creativity and considerable skills.

How Do You Hit A Fade And Then A Draw?

One of the first questions we ask any player we are working with is: "Does the swing create the shot or does the shot create the swing?"

More often than not, the initially reply is: "Well, the swing creates the shot of course."

We generally let them think about that for a minute or two then ask if they would use the same swing to hit a high fade as they would for a low draw. It doesn't take long for them to realise that their initial reaction wasn't perhaps the right one. The penny drops, the light bulb goes on and a sheepish grin spreads across their face.

"Well, I know I have to swing in to out with the clubface closed to the path to hit a draw and I have to swing out to in with the face open to the path to hit a fade, so the two swings have to be slightly different in order to hit the two different shots."

We then ask them to hit these two shots. Straight away, the way they set up to hit the high fade and low draw are noticeably different. We then show them on video how slightly different the two swings look and, using TrackMan, highlight just how different their impact conditions – club path, angle of attack and face-to-path relationship are.

When you think about it logically, it seems unrealistic and almost nonsensical to expect the same swing to produce two very different shots. Yet when you go for a golf lesson or go to the range you will almost always do so in order to work on your swing. Would it not make more sense to work on creating shots rather than trying to create or recreate a consistent swing?

If you visit the driving range at any professional tour event around the world, pay attention to the ball flight of the shots they hit. You will see the players hitting fairly similar shots, whether they be soft fades, gentle draws, or straight bullets.

Now take a look at the swings that create these shots. The shots may be similar but the swings or styles that create them are very, very different. The players' focused attention is very much on what the ball has to do to reach its intended target.

Think about all other ball sports. Tennis, football, soccer, rugby, squash, cricket – the list goes on. Where would your attention be playing any of these sports? Correct, the ball. So why would golf be any different?

Neglect the ball and its importance at your peril.

Why Consistency Is Over-rated
(And Barely Exists, Even At Tour Level)

On the surface, Brooks Koepka's 2018 scoring average of 69.4 was extremely consistent. However, this graph shows how that stroke average was achieved. Consistent? We'll let you draw your own conclusions.

Brooks Koepka's 2018 Scores

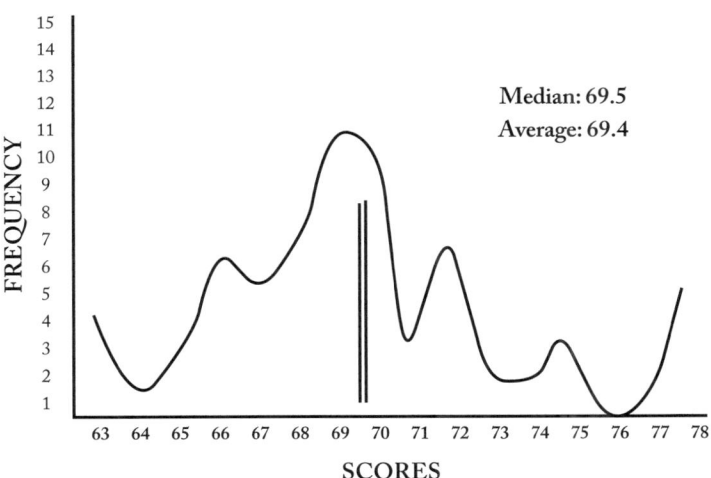

Graph courtesy of Trent Wearner Golf

You will have gathered by now that the concept of consistency is overrated and virtually unachievable, so it makes no sense to waste valuable time and effort chasing that impossible dream.

What does consistency look like anyway?

In 2018, Brooks Koepka won two Majors, over $7million and was, for a spell, the No 1 ranked golfer on the planet. He played in 17 PGA Tour events, made 15 cuts, recorded 10 top 10s and finished 3rd in the FedEx Cup rankings.

Pretty consistent, right? On the surface, absolutely. His results certainly were. However, if you dig a little deeper, you will find that his scores throughout the season weren't quite as consistent as you might think.

Think about your lowest and highest scores in competitions over the last year. How many shots separated your lowest and highest scores – eight, 10, 12?

For Koepka, that number was 15. No that is not a typo – it was 15.

His lowest score was 63 (which he shot four times) and his highest was 78 (which he shot five times).

His stroke average was 69.4 over the course of the season, which would suggest consistent play, but we're pretty sure Koepka wouldn't necessarily see his scoring as consistent.

Was his swing inconsistent and varying massively on a daily or weekly basis? A little, yes. A lot, no. As hard and as smart as he works with his coach Claude Harmon, we doubt it changed a whole lot.

Were other aspects of his game, like short game, putting, his mental state and the way he was feeling physically on certain days changeable throughout that period? Almost certainly.

Interestingly, Koepka is a player who likes to keep things simple; who, in his own words, tries to "make it a reaction sport instead of trying to fundamentally think about everything. I think you can get caught up in trying to put your swing here or there or whatever, but it's never going to be in the same place two days in a row. It might look it but it's never going to be exactly the same." By the middle of 2019, Koepka had won four majors, been World No 1 and won golf tournaments all over the world. He is clearly a very smart guy who has figured out what works for him.

Improve Your Skills, Not Your Swing

Yes, we want to help you play better golf on a more regular basis. However, expecting your body to recreate the exact same swing, time after time, is, in all likelihood, unrealistic.

Better scores come from learning and implementing better skills, not necessarily from making better (which is largely subjective anyway) swings.

Golfers often talk about consistency and yet they think they will find it through constant change. Work that one out.

We're not saying technique isn't important. Good technique will provide a more solid platform than poor technique.

Perhaps Jack Nicklaus, the record major-winner of all time, summed it up perfectly when he said: "I feel that hitting specific shots, playing the ball to a certain place in a certain way, is 50 per cent mental picture, 40 per cent set up and 10 per cent swing."

With 18 Majors on his CV, it's tough to argue against that kind of thinking. Jack used visualisation techniques on all his shots and said: "I never hit a bad shot in my mind before I hit it."

In other words, he always had a very clear picture of what a good shot looked like. We doubt very much if he ever saw a shot coming up 30 yards short of a green or careering out of bounds from the tee in his mind's eye before he played a particular shot at any given time. There is some very strong scientific evidence to support his theories into which we will delve a little deeper later in the book.

Something that we have discovered in our coaching in recent years using TrackMan to measure what the golf ball does, is that while shot patterns may vary with most players, their swing patterns are less likely to vary.

When we say swing patterns, we mean specifically swing path and swing direction.

Without getting too technical, when we ask a player to hit, say, three shots to a specific target with the same club, regardless of their playing ability, more often than not, the variability in their swing path/swing direction is rarely more than two or three degrees, which would not be visible to the naked eye.

While there may be as much as 30 or 40 yards difference left and right, and long and short, of their intended target, that inconsistency is not down to the player's swing changing from shot to shot.

While your golf swing may feel very different to how it did on the previous week, day or even hole, your swing patterns will not vary nearly as much as the way you feel from day to day, or how your emotions or emotional reactions will fluctuate.

Nine times out of 10, the inconsistency in distance and direction is down to one of a few things:

• Whether you have a clear intention of what that shot will look and feel like
• Where the club face is pointing at impact
• Where the ball is struck on the clubface

How do we know this? Quite simply because unless you have a clear intention, anything can and will happen. Furthermore, we now have the technology to measure the other two parameters. This eliminates any kind of guesswork and having to make up stories about how the player 'came over the top' on the shot that went left or 'got ahead of' the shot that went right. This is what tends to happen when a TV commentator's producer is screaming into his earpiece asking him to explain what happened and why the last shot was hooked or blocked.

When Did You Last Pay Attention To Your Ball-Striking?

Most golfers are a whole lot better at controlling or repeating their swing than they think they are, which is enormously reassuring for them. Unfortunately, the flip side of that is that they are generally a whole lot worse at controlling the clubface and hitting the ball out the sweet spot than they think they are.

Think about this for a moment: when was the last time you actually paid any attention to where the face was pointing at the moment of contact or where you hit the ball on the clubface?

With modern golf clubs promising more forgiveness than ever before, our attention has shifted away from striking the ball out the middle of the clubface. We live in a golfing world where distance is everything and golfers obsess about clubhead speed.

However, clubhead speed doesn't tell the full story about how far you hit the ball.

If you are at all technologically minded as a golfer, you are probably aware of the term 'smash factor', which is ball speed divided by clubhead speed.

Smash factor is essentially a measurement of efficiency.

We have seen high club speeds with relatively low ball speeds and the golf ball flying all over the place and, conversely, relatively low clubhead speeds producing high ball speeds and excellent golf shots.

The difference? Where the ball is struck on the face.

Most golfers who struggle to strike the ball out of the middle of the club tend to do so for one simple reason. They simply don't pay any attention to it.

When was the last time you actually paid attention to hitting the ball out the middle of the golf club – been a while?

Anyone who grew up playing blades and persimmon woods will know all about the importance of a centred strike. For those of you who haven't enjoyed that experience, we strongly suggest you do. You will very, very quickly become acutely aware of what both a sweet spot strike and an off-centre strike feel like.

While we would all love to have a technically sound, aesthetically pleasing golf swing, let's not focus our attention on form at the expense of function.

We all know the guy with the beautiful golf swing who can't hit it worth a lick and we all know his friend who swings it 'awful' but hits it out the middle and hits way more fairways and greens than we think he should.

Since the introduction of shot tracker graphics on TV, it's interesting to hear people saying things like 'did you see the flight on that drive Rory hit?' and 'did you see how low Tiger's stinger went?'

Before we had shot tracker graphics to feast our eyes on, we were talking about backswing positions and voicing opinions on the merits of whichever player's swing.

As far as we are concerned, this can only be a good thing. It directs our attention to the shot, which is unique to that player and that unique moment in time.

The player's intention of what shot they want to play will determine the move they make with their body and the golf club. The shot is what matters most. The shot is king.

The Difference Between A Swing And A Shot

Ben Hogan has long been recognised as the golfer with the 'best' swing in the history of the game. So much so that Jack Nicklaus would always stop to watch him hit shots every opportunity.

What has been lost in the Hogan mystique over the years is that he was also one of the greatest shotmakers who worked tirelessly on controlling his golf ball. As a result, he developed a technique admired by all.

We have seen far too many golfers of all standards falling into the trap of seeking perfection through science and endlessly performing backswing drills in order to get the club "in the slot". What we have found from our own experience, and we have since found scientific evidence to support our findings, is that when you break down the golf swing into parts or segments, it simply doesn't work.

At a recent golf school we were hosting at Archerfield, one very good player told us she was working on her backswing and the videos she had seen of her swing would suggest that she was making progress.

That being the case, we asked her to hit the next three shots, placing her attention entirely on her backswing. Once she had addressed the ball and taken to the club up to the top of her backswing, she stopped, looked at us and asked: "What do I do now?"

It was only then that she realised that her brain had figured out that she had achieved her goal of performing the task of 'making a good backswing' and had essentially switched off and thought 'mission accomplished'.

Essentially, as soon as she had completed her backswing, her attention would wander somewhere else. It certainly wasn't on creating the shot, simply because her attention was never really on the shot in the first instance. Only when your attention is on the shot you want to create do you realistically have any chance of having any influence on it.

One story which really resonated with us and we are sure will strike a chord with you is that of our good friend and Sky Sports commentator Andrew Coltart. Andrew is a former European Tour player who has won on three different continents and played against Tiger Woods in the 1999 Ryder Cup.

On Karl's The Brain Booster podcast, Coltart spoke very openly and honestly about the struggles he endured in the latter part of his career. He had reached a point where he felt he had to improve his swing and sought out a well-known swing coach.

Andrew said: "I invested a lot of time and money in a bid to gain a better golf swing. After numerous lessons and endless hours on the range working on positions, I wasn't seeing any signs of improvement. In fact I got worse – a lot worse.

"So much so that I got to the point where I remember playing in a European Tour event at Gleneagles and I hit a tee shot 70 yards out of bounds. I was a better golfer as a 12-year-old than I was at that stage. It was embarrassing. I had lost all confidence in my ability to play golf. I had become so clouded with trying to put the club in certain positions, that I had forgotten what a good shot actually looked like. I was in a very dark place for quite some time as an awful lot of mental scar tissue had developed.

"Eventually I had to re-trace my steps, have a complete mental de-clutter and went back to playing the game the way I had previously, shaping shots this way and that.

"I went back to playing golf not golf swing.

"If I could go back in time, I would spend more time actually playing golf on the course than hitting balls on the range. I would play golf and have fun in the process. I would work on becoming better at what I did naturally, not work on what a golf coach's idea of what a good swing looked like.

"Golf swings are like fingerprints, unique to the individual and should be viewed and treated as such. You just need to look at guys like Dustin Johnson, Jim Furyk and Rickie Fowler – the list is endless. They have found their way of playing the game and playing it extremely well.

"The golf swing to me is at most 10 per cent of the equation. All the other ingredients such as course management, confidence, self-esteem, the way you talk to and about yourself are all so important.

"It wasn't until after I had retired from tournament golf that I really understood that "my" golf swing basically couldn't produce wild shots. That isn't an opinion, it's a fact. Having hit numerous shots with a variety of clubs using TrackMan to gather data on my impact conditions and ball flight, I discovered that my swing was actually very reliable.

"If only I had been armed with that information and knowledge I would have hit the ball harder, probably a lot further and wouldn't have worried about positions and what my swing looked like," he said.

There is a valuable lesson for us all there. Yes we can learn from our own mistakes but we can also avoid a lot of potential heartache by learning from other people's experiences.

Again, we are not suggesting that technique has no importance. However, if all you are working on is how your swing looks and not the shots it creates, then you may eventually or occasionally see some benefit but the reality is that if you are not paying attention to the shot itself your progress and development as a golfer will be slow and probably painful.

On the flip side, if you pay more attention to creating shots – and, after all, that is what the golf course and its designer are asking of you – not only will you become better at performing that specific task but also, time after time, we see golf swings improving as a direct result.

How does this happen? Fundamentally, your brain and body will figure out what needs to happen in order to create the shot you are faced with once you have a very clear picture of what that good shot looks like.

You will soon figure out the best way to create that shot and your body will move in a certain way as a direct consequence. More often than not, this will look and feel 'like it should'.

In other words, you will find the 'positions' you have been searching for without trying to place the club or specific parts of your body there.

Just like hitting a nail into a piece of wood, the task creates the technique. Cause and effect.

Think about it this way. If we were to give you a tennis racquet and throw a ball to you and ask you to hit it high to the right, low to the left or straight ahead of you, your body would move in three different ways, according to what your intention is.

Your attention would very probably be on the racquet and where you want the ball to go, not on your backswing, shoulder turn or weight transference. The shot you wanted to create would determine how your body moved.

As we mentioned earlier, this logic applies in pretty much every other ball sport, so why would golf be any different?

Your golf clubs are the tools of your trade. Learn how to use them in order to create the shot or shots you visualise. Remember this, regardless of how much money you spend on a new driver, set of irons, wedge or a putter, one thing you will not get as part of the deal is a user's manual.

Your golf clubs are the best training aids you could possibly buy, so make sure:

- They are right for you
- You learn how to apply the club in a certain way to create a certain shot

Tiger's 15th Major – And His Amazing Shot-Making

This book would not be complete without a special mention of Tiger's incredible victory at Augusta in April 2019.

Very few people in the golfing world thought this possible only two or three years prior to this historic event. With various, knee and back surgeries, an apparent inability to get the ball close to the hole from around the greens and a world ranking outside the top 1,000, it was widely thought that Tiger was finished. He was past his best. He would never win another tournament, never mind another Major. In late 2016, early 2017, he could barely walk and needed help to get out of bed in the mornings.

What the golf world didn't count on was Tiger's desire and determination to work as hard and as smart as he had ever done in a bid to firstly compete and ultimately to win again. He had shown some signs of form throughout 2018, culminating in a victory in the Tour Championships at East Lake, Atlanta, where the crowds cheering him on down the 72nd hole were quite astonishing. The roar that went up as he holed the winning putt was almost deafening but that was nothing compared to what would happen just over six months later at the Masters.

Going into the final round two shots behind the reigning Open Champion Francesco Molinari, Tiger could potentially do the unimaginable. He could win a major at the age of 43, a full 11 years after winning his last one, the 2008 US Open, and 22 years after his first Masters win.

It has often been said that the Masters doesn't really begin until the back nine on Sunday. It may sound a bit of a cliché but how true that turned out to be. With the lead changing hands what appeared to be every time you looked at the leaderboard, Woods produced an absolute masterclass in shotmaking and how to get the job done.

While all those around him became aware of the magnitude of what they might achieve, Tiger got on with the task at hand which was to create and produce one shot at a time.

Talk about creativity – he hit low stinger 3-woods, high fades, low draws, with the touch of a Bond Street pickpocket on and around the greens. Tiger did it all. His mental strength and ability to keep his focused attention on each and every shot was quite remarkable. He was unquestionably 'in the zone.'

TV commentators such as former Ryder Cup Captain Paul McGinley and three-time major winner Padraig Harrington, both very astute men, constantly talked about Tiger's shot selection, creativity and execution.

It was perhaps the first time in decades that virtually nobody was analysing and dissecting his swing.

As you can imagine, this was music to our ears. Golf swings don't win tournaments, golfers do.

Shot after shot, hole after hole, he quite simply created the right shot at the right time. When others were firing at flags and finding watery graves, more often than not, Woods played the smart shot to the correct side of the fairway and the wide part of the green.

Through a combination of experience, wisdom, sheer talent and basically knowing what shot to play when, Tiger emerged triumphant. In what has been described as the greatest sporting comeback of all time, Tiger put golf on the front and back pages of newspapers and magazines.

TV and radio broadcasts around the world opened with scenes of him celebrating like we've never seen before. Tiger Woods is box office. He is still the biggest attraction in golf.

His former coach of many years, Butch Harmon said: "Jack Nicklaus may well be the greatest champion of all time but I believe Tiger is the greatest golfer the game has ever seen."

Thank you, Tiger. Hopefully your endeavours will inspire yet another generation of young golfers to get out on the golf courses of the world.

Regardless of your age and current standard of play, take a leaf out of Tiger's book and go out there and create shots. Did you see how much fun he was having?

You owe it to yourself as a golfer to try creating different shots. What's the worst that can happen? View every shot as a unique opportunity to create something special.

If it doesn't quite work out, learn from it and take that learning with you. Next time you are faced with a similar shot, or any shot for that matter, you will be better equipped to turn your visualisation into a real-life creation of that very shot. Is it possible that the next shot you hit could be the best you have ever played? Absolutely.

Tiger showed the world what is indeed possible and we thank him once more for that.

Shane Lowry – Open champion And Golfing Artist

While we are on the topic of winning major championships, let's turn our attention to the 148th Open Championship at Royal Portrush in July 2019. Testing conditions are almost always guaranteed as the weather can and does change in a heartbeat in that part of the world. The players who adapted and adjusted best to these conditions were bound to be at the top of the famous yellow scoreboard after 72 holes.

Royal Portrush is a shot-maker's paradise so, on reflection, it shouldn't have come as too much of a surprise to see Irishman Shane Lowry come out on top.

For those of you who have had the pleasure of watching Shane play, you will be well aware of his razor-sharp short game and his ability to control his golf ball in all kinds of conditions.

He can and did hit a variety of shots: high, low, left to right, right to left and occasionally dead straight. You name it, he did it and he did it when it mattered en route to an incredibly impressive six-shot victory. For those of you who haven't seen him in action, take time to do so in the future, it really is a joy and a pleasure to watch, admire and learn from.

Lowry clearly has a great feel for the game and a fantastic imagination to match his considerable skills.

After lifting the famous Claret Jug, he said: "I play the game the way I see it. There are times when I'm not playing great and thinking too many technical thoughts. But if someone asks me how to hit a fade, my artistic side takes over. I think 'fade' and hit a fade."

He was very quick to thank his caddie, Brian 'Bo' Martin, who could be heard throughout the last round saying: "Stay with me, Shane, stay with me."

Bo, who is a long time friend of ours, wasn't talking about Shane keeping pace with him as they walked down the fairways. He was bringing his man back to the present moment, enabling him to focus on the task at hand, one shot at a time.

He could see Lowry getting ahead of himself and thinking about the consequences of potentially winning golf's greatest prize.

Asking him to "stay with me" was Bo's way of bringing him back to the here and now and directing his attention to the next shot. This allowed Lowry to do what he does best: creating the right shot at the right time.

It would be fair to say that Shane Lowry, champion golfer of the year in 2019, totally 'gets' the art of playing golf.

Key Takeaways

1 Instead of asking 'what is wrong with my swing', ask 'what is wrong with my shots'.

2 Work on creating shots rather than trying to replicate a consistent swing.

3 The concept of consistency is overrated and virtually unachievable – even for tour players.

4 Better scores come from learning and implementing better skills, not necessarily from making better swings.

5 When did you last pay attention to where the clubface was pointing at the moment of contact or where you hit the ball on the clubface?

6 Only when your attention is on the shot you want to create do you realistically have any chance of making it happen.

7 Tiger won the 2019 Masters with his shotmaking and strategy not on account of how he was swinging the club.

8 Shane Lowry, the 2019 Open champion, says he hits a fade by thinking about a fade.

THE LATE, GREAT SEVE BALLESTEROS

We'd like to pay tribute to the greatest golfing artist of them all. Seve exemplified how the shot creates the swing

Gary On Seve

THE late, great Severiano Ballesteros, perhaps the finest example of a creative, artistic shotmaker and entertainer extraordinaire, sadly fell victim to the search for perfection.

In his prime, Seve missed his fair share of fairways and greens but more than made up for that with spectacular recovery shots from parts of the golf course that were deemed unnecessary to be included in most yardage charts.

His imagination, creativity and feel, allied to an incredible amount of natural talent, allowed Seve to play shots that most of his peers couldn't even dream of. Those attributes were even considered an unfair advantage by many of his contemporaries.

I was lucky enough to meet the great man, when my late father Alister, a well known golf writer, took me to meet Seve at the Open Championship at Muirfield in 1980.

Seve had won the Open at Royal Lytham & St. Annes the previous year, earning the label of 'the car park champion' along the way due to hitting a few errant tee shots that week.

He had also recently become the proud owner of a Green Jacket, having won the Masters only a few months earlier.

I remember as a 12-year-old boy being extremely excited and nervous in equal measure as we walked on to the range and I was introduced to this guy who I had only ever seen on TV and read about in the newspapers.

He had the whitest shoes and the biggest smile I had ever seen. He spoke to me for about five minutes, asking how my game was, what was my handicap and was I enjoying my golf? It felt like he was speaking to me not as a child but as a golfer. That was it, I was hooked. I was even more of a bona fide Seve fan from that day on. We watched him hit shots for about half an hour and I was transfixed. In awe of how effortless it looked.

I knew nothing about the golf swing back then but I did know mine looked nothing like his.

More importantly, he was making the ball do things that I had never, ever seen before.

Flighting shots high and low, hitting fades and draws, you name it, he was doing it and apparently having a lot of fun in the process. And this was just a warm-up for a Tuesday practice round.

It wasn't until many years later, I truly understood why he was hitting all these different shots on the range. He was playing shots on the range that he figured he would have to play on the course. He clearly knew that the golf course would demand that he hit certain shots in certain winds on certain holes.

I wasn't really aware of it at the time but my guess is that most of the other guys on the range were probably working on their backswings and trying to hit it as straight as they could, time after time. I wasn't interested in what they were doing, I was absorbed in watching Seve the artist in the flesh with my own eyes.

I had seen one of golf's true global superstars creating all sorts of shots without doing any drills, checking where his club was in P1 or P2 or at the top of the backswing – none of that nonsense.

His attention was on the golf ball and what he wanted it to do. What an education.

I wanted to be Seve but I'm pretty sure I wasn't alone in that respect – he was an inspiration for a generation.

In stark contrast, wind the clock forward to the Open at Turnberry in 1994. I was coaching a couple of players on tour by then and when one of the guys I was working with wanted to hit balls, I was duly sent to find a spot on the range.

Being Tuesday, it was very, very busy and the only spot was between Seve and Bernhard Langer. I remember vividly how Seve was struggling to keep the ball on the range, so God only knows how he was going to keep it on the golf course.

He was working on this position and that position and had got to the point where he would listen to virtually anyone with an opinion on what he should do with his swing. If it broke my heart to witness this, I can only imagine what it was doing to my hero.

I wouldn't say he had gone but he certainly didn't have the same aura of the great champion I had first met in 1980.

While he still went on to do great things, it was sad to see his demise at close quarters.

I often wonder what might have been had Seve gone back to being Seve the creative artist and not tried to become a swing technician. Sadly he was no longer playing golf but was trying to play golf swing. He was looking for *the* way rather than going back to and trusting *his* way.

I don't believe for a second that he had lost his swing but I do believe he had lost the feel of his swing.

Furthermore, his attention was now much more focused on what he was doing with his golf swing rather than what he was doing with his golf ball.

Seve's Greatest shot – At The 1983 Ryder Cup

In 1983, watching the Ryder Cup at PGA National in Florida, I was one of relatively few, very fortunate people on the entire planet who witnessed what Jack Nicklaus described as 'the greatest shot I ever saw', writes Gary.

In an interview with the Telegraph some 28 years later, Seve's Ryder Cup team-mate Bernhard Langer described it perfectly.

"He hit his second shot in a bunker at the par 5 last, having missed the fairway with his drive," said Langer. "I had finished my match and went out to watch. I was thinking that I would use a 7-iron to clear the lip and lay up for a wedge or 9-iron into the green.

"Seve had 245 yards to the front edge of the green. There was water everywhere and the lip was so high. Save pulled out his 3-wood and I thought: what is he going to do with that? The ball was in the sand a few feet away from a two-foot lip. Then I saw the most amazing shot I have ever seen. He didn't just clear the lip, he drew the ball, starting it out over the lake and onto the green and made an incredible par.

"This, to me, is still the most miraculous shot I have ever seen. He was a magician with a golf club," said Langer.

A stunned Fuzzy Zoeller, Seve's opponent that day, said shortly after: "They say great golfers make great shots but that one made me blink!"

Karl On Seve

BOTH Gary and I come from a generation of golfers who were hugely influenced by the great Spanish golfing genius Severiano Ballesteros. It is our hope in some small way this book keeps some of those glorious memories burning for a future generation. We both feel intense sadness that young players today may lose touch with Seve and his legacy. He was truly the ultimate golfing artist. At his best he embodied the art of playing golf.

For many the first experience of his genius was back in 1976 at the Open held at Royal Birkdale. As a relatively unknown, 19-year-old rookie he announced himself to the golfing world. One shot in particular gave us a hint of the artistry that would mesmerize golfing audiences around the world for the next twenty years or so. 1976 was known as the 'fiery summer' because of the endless sunny days. Week after week of blazing sun had left golf courses up and down the British Isles tinder-dry.

At the start of the last round Seve had gone out in the final group with the eventual champion Johnny Miller who played a stunning final round of 66 to win. However Seve came up the last hole with Miller needing a birdie four to tie with Jack Nicklaus for second place. A pulled second shot left him with an almost impossible pitch to a pin tucked tight on the left hand side of the green.

The standard, floated pitch would have left him twenty feet from the flag at the very best.

The young Spaniard surveyed the scene and suddenly he had seen the opportunity to create a shot. There was a possibility to run the ball through a tiny gap between the bunkers.

The margin for error was at best a couple of inches either side.

But Seve's imagination had seen it. The shot that began in his creative imagination drew gasps of amazement as he played a perfect pitch and run through the tiny gap and the ball came to rest five feet from the flag.

Of course, Seve tapped in the putt to tie Nicklaus but such was the audacity of the shot Miller actually commented upon it in his winning acceptance speech. If you get the chance look up the clip on YouTube and let your jaw drop at the sheer wizardry as Seve's mind combined with the skill in his body to produce a shot that will be remembered forever.

My first memory of Seve was at the very same venue Royal Birkdale seven years later in 1983 in the Open won by Tom Watson.

I was stood at the back of the second tee at the beginning of the first practice round.

Over thirty years later I still have an image seared in my mind of Seve walking to the tee.

His presence was electric. I remember vividly he was wearing a pair of black slacks matched with a white Slazenger sweater, and his FootJoy shoes glistened with pristine newness.

He dropped a couple of balls onto the immaculate turf and again if I close my eyes I can see and hear that shot as he drilled a 2-iron right down the middle of the fairway.

The sound of club meeting ball was like the crack of a whip.

To an impressionable sixteen-year-old mind this was truly what a hero looked like.

I've spent time talking to legendary tour caddie Billy Foster and he regaled us with numerous stories of the great five years he spent on Seve's bag.

Billy felt that, above all else, his ability to create golf shots was his most valuable weapon.

He talked in particular about the famous shot he hit on the final hole at Crans sur Sierre to win the European Masters in 1990. The great man was five shots of the lead with six holes to play. He proceeded to birdie 13, 14, 15 16 and 17 but then on the last hole he carved his tee shot way off into the trees on the right.

Billy talks about the next shot as, in his opinion, being perhaps the greatest golf shot ever played. Seve was behind a wall, in the trees with literally no shot to play. His caddie tried to advise him to just chip out and aim to make a par.

Seve was having none of it. "Go away, Billy, I have the shot," he said'. Foster was dispatched from the scene. The next thing I heard was a swish of the club and out came this missile from in the trees and somehow Ballesteros had managed to get the ball to the front of the green. Billy Foster is adamant that nobody else would have even contemplated that shot.

To round off a perfect story, Seve then chipped the next shot into the hole to seal a truly remarkable victory.

According to Foster the will to win Seve had was something to behold. Growing up in Pedrena in northern Spain he had a very poor upbringing and initially learned to play the game as a caddie.

He made his own golf club with a 3-iron head and honed his game playing shots on the beach.

Many years later, I saw Seve give an instruction clinic and he was playing the most beautiful flop shots out of a bunker with a 3-iron. He gave other pros the opportunity to try these shots but nobody could come close to him.

Can you imagine how easy it must have seemed to Seve when he actually got to play the game with a full set of wedges?

Billy told me that in his 35 years of caddying all over the world and on every major tour the only player who has come even remotely close to Seve's short game has been Phil Mickelson.

It was so very sad to see Seve's game take a steep decline in his late thirties. Billy saw this decline at first hand. In his opinion, the once glorious natural talent became dulled as a result of Seve taking so much instruction and looking to improve his swing.

In his own inimitable way Foster said: "At one time he had more coaches than Wallace Arnold."

Seve would literally take advice from anyone. In effect, he began to ask 'what is wrong with my swing' instead of 'what is wrong with my shots'.

The greatest shotmaker this game has ever known destroyed his game in the search for better technique.

Even as his game declined rapidly he could still, when the situation demanded, use his unbelievable recovery skills to perform miracles. Who can ever forget his Ryder Cup singles match in 1995 against Tom Lehman? The American was at the height of his powers and split every fairway and hit every green. Seve hit the ball sideways and was all over the golf course but somehow he managed to stay with Lehman until late in the game through sheer tenacity and some unbelievable recovery play. The look on Lehman's face in the midst of it all was something to behold.

However, Seve had lost his game forever. He never recovered. He drowned in technique at the expense of his genius to play shots.

I asked Billy what his number-one recommendation would be to young players aiming to get better at the game.

In a heartbeat, he simply suggested to get out on the golf course with just a few clubs and learn to create different shots. Even to go out and play with just one club and learn what you can do when you become absorbed in creating this shot in this moment. Engaging more of your creativity and imagination and less of your intellect.

What we have found is that to do this late at night with the course to yourself is to immerse yourself in an almost spiritual experience.

You are creating shots for their own sake. You will tune back into some of the very core reasons why you began to play the game in the first place.

Seve was with us for too short a time yet he inspired so many. He was a true golfing legend in a world where the very word legend has been dulled to the extremes of pointlessness.

Chapter 4
WHAT DOES A GOOD SHOT LOOK LIKE?

Only when you have clear intention can you begin to create the shot you want to hit

Visualisation / vɪʒ(j)ʊəlʌɪˈzeɪʃ(ə)n / Noun. The formation of a mental image of something.

WE create what we see. Is it possible that you could hit a good shot? Is it possible that the next shot you hit will be the best one you have ever hit in your life? What does the ball need to do to reach your intended target? What does a good shot look like?

Before you hit any shot, whether that be on the range or the golf course, whether it is with a driver, a 6-iron or even a three-foot putt, it is essential that you have a very clear picture of what the very best version of that shot looks like. Once you have a very clear intention, you then have somewhere specific to place your attention.

We are not going to suggest that everyone visualises every shot exactly the same way.

Some golfers see the ball flying towards their intended target with a high fade, others with a low draw. Some even see the ball flying arrow-straight towards its intended destination.

A lot depends on what shot is required, what shot you are capable of playing and what shot you are most comfortable with at that unique moment in time. A lot depends on your intention.

Just a quick word of warning for those who are trying to hit the ball dead straight every time. If hitting arrow-straight shots is your expectation, be prepared for a lifetime of disappointment.

From the data we have gathered from hundreds of thousands of shots using TrackMan which tracks the flight of the ball from start to finish, we could count the number of full shots with zero curvature on one hand. Even shots that look dead straight will have some amount of curvature or shape. If you can understand and accept that, disappointment will not be an issue.

We are not saying that straight isn't a shape or an option when it comes to visualising and creating shots.

In fact, the feedback we have received from a number of good players is that the idea of 'straight is a shape' works well for them in the sense that if they commit to a shot and it moves a little either way, they are never too far away from their intended target.

Our ultimate aim is to help you to discover, or perhaps rediscover, your way.

If this currently works for you, keep doing it. Golf is a game of options and with a little experimentation, you will soon start to see which option or options work best for you on the golf course.

If you aren't 100 per cent sure of what your tendencies are – fades, draws or straight shots – we strongly recommend you have a session with a qualified and experienced launch monitor operator.

They will not form an opinion but they will provide you with accurate and helpful data based on the shots you hit. Once you know your tendencies, you will have a very clear picture of what you can and cannot do.

Knowing what you are capable of in your golf game is very important but knowing what you cannot do will really enable you to develop and progress on your journey to becoming the best possible golfer you can be.

Modern golf clubs are designed to create a high launch, low spin ball flight to maximise distance with golf balls that are designed to do something similar.

As a result, if the golf ball is spinning less, ie creating less backspin, there will also be less 'sidespin'.

Technically, sidespin doesn't actually exist. If the ball curves left or right, the reality is that the ball is spinning on a tilted axis due to the face being open or closed to the path or the ball being struck towards the heel or toe, creating gear effect.

There is some fantastic information on this at trackmangolf.com which we recommend you look at to help you gain a comprehensive understanding of the ball flight laws.

While modern clubs and golf balls generate less spin, they do still generate a certain amount of spin. There is a bit of a myth about spin and that less spin is always better.

Without an element of spin, the golf ball would fall out of the air like a wounded duck. Some top players prefer a ball that spins more because it allows them to shape their shots more easily. If you tend to create a lot of spin or, in your mind, too much spin, it might be worth experimenting with different types of golf ball.

Better still, visit an expert pro, coach or club fitter and go through a ball fitting process. Yes, ball fitting.

Most golfers are aware of the importance of having their clubs fitted to suit their game but how have you ever considered going for a ball fitting to suit your style of play?

Think about it logically. If your intention is to create shots with a minimal amount of curvature and you are using a relatively high-spinning ball 'because the pros use this ball', you are, in effect, making your task harder than it need be.

Conversely, if your intention is to create shots with a lot of shape and you are using a relatively low-spinning ball then, again, you are making your task all the more difficult.

Essentially, the amount the ball spins will influence the amount the ball curves which in turn influences how you visualise and ultimately play your intended shots. Regardless of the shot you want to create, you must be clear that your intention is to hit a good shot rather than to try not to hit a bad shot.

If we said 'whatever you do, don't think about a bright red sports car' what is the first image that appears in your mind's eye? Perhaps you can tell us how that Ferrari looks?

Believe In Science – But Be Careful

We have said from the outset that our belief is that the game of golf has become way too scientific and we are drowning in scientific information which can lead to an unnecessary amount of mental clutter. This gets in the way of our natural ability to create good golf shots. If your attention is on your wrist angles at the top of the backswing, your transfer of pressure in the downswing or whether your left wrist has sufficient supination or flexion through impact, you can't possibly be paying attention to the actual shot and the art of creating it.

As far as we know, when you fill in your scorecard, you are asked how many shots you hit, not how many swings you made or how these swings looked. That's why they give you a pencil and not a box of crayons to fill in you card. As the old saying goes: "There are no pictures on the scorecard."

However, we are not dismissing science. Far from it. In fact we look to science in our research to back up our beliefs and personal findings. This research has led us down many paths and, at the end of one particular path, we found a fascinating book by Bill Bodri called Visualisation Power.

We have long believed that visualisation is an essential tool golfers should add to their skillset if they are ever to achieve their goals and fulfil their potential. Bodri says: "Visualisation skills, which are the power to form stable mental images in your mind, are used everywhere in highly competitive sports by top performing athletes."

We know from our own personal experience of working with thousands of golfers over the last 30 years that those who have the ability to imagine a crystal-clear mental picture of the shots they intend to create, also have the greatest potential and ability to bring these shots to life.

Bodri goes on: "Mentally training your powers of visualisation will not only develop your concentration skills, such as the ability to ignore distractions, but also your powers of discipline and the ability to focus."

These comments are not just theories dreamt up in a laboratory but are based on the findings of numerous scientific experiments, many involving Olympic athletes.

One such study was conducted by the sports psychologist Richard Suinn. A group of skiers were wired to special EMG (electromyography) equipment to test their neuromuscular responses while they were carrying out their mental skiing rehearsals. The results were astonishing.

"As the skiers mentally rehearsed downhill runs in their minds, visualising everything they must do to run a successful course, the electrical impulses heading to their muscles while visualising were found to be the same as those they used in real life while actually skiing the run," said Suinn.

"Even though the skiers weren't moving, the exact same muscles they would have used during a downhill ski were being activated because of using their minds."

From Suinn's findings, and those of others, we have learned that strong visualisation of the shot, the movement you make in order to create that shot and how you react to that shot, create very strong neural pathways.

In other words, you are creating a mental blueprint in your brain. This in turn enables your actions, movements and reactions to become more automatic. The more automatic these actions and reactions become, the less room and time there is for unnecessary and unhelpful mental clutter to develop.

We have referenced the great Jack Nicklaus elsewhere in this book and make no apologies for doing so again. We both remember as kids eager to learn from the best reading his best-selling book Golf My Way, which was originally printed in 1974.

One stand-out quote reads: "I never hit a shot, even in practice, without having a sharp in-focus picture of it in my head.

"It's like a colour movie. First I see the ball where I want it to finish, nice and white sitting up on the bright green grass. Then the scene quickly changes and I see the ball going there: its path, trajectory and shape, even its behaviour on landing.

"Then there's a sort of fade-out and the next scene shows me making the kind of swing that will turn the previous images into reality and only at the end of this short, private Hollywood spectacular, do I select a club and set up to the ball."

Talk about clarity! What is really fascinating here is that Jack has watched the whole movie before he has even selected a club. What we see at all levels, from weekend golfers to Tour Pros, is the player taking a club out of their bag because the shot they face is x yards, make a couple of practice swings and only then look at their target and try to create a mental image of the shot they are about to create. The sequence of events is somewhat different. Perhaps Mr Nicklaus was onto something all those years ago.

What the Golden Bear doesn't mention is what triggered that sequence of events. If you are one of our more observant readers, you will have picked up on the fact that we like to ask questions.

Questions focus the mind.

The 2010 US Open champion Graeme McDowell once told us that 'questions are indeed the answer'.

Could it be that Jack Nicklaus was asking himself the all-important question 'what does a good shot look like' as the trigger to start the movie in his mind?

Seve Ballesteros, as his former caddie Billy Foster mentioned in the previous chapter, was never the straightest of hitters and as a result often found himself in some unusual parts of the golf course.

We have all been there, and isn't it strange that when we have to shape a shot around a tree or create one with a lot of curve or height, we somehow manage to see that shot with amazing clarity?

In the book, Natural Golf, Seve said: "When in trouble, I always stand directly behind the ball, stare intently at my target and wait patiently for the movies to begin. Sometimes I see so many shots come to life that I think I'm looking into a kaleidoscope. When that happens, I stay in the same spots and I rerun all the options until I see one working better than the others. Then, and only then, do I visualise the specific swing needed to execute the shot and finally select the proper club for the task."

There are a few very important things to pay attention to here. Seve had an incredible imagination and was very aware of his target. He waited until he saw 'the' shot. He then visualised and probably felt the specific swing required and then, finally, he selected the appropriate tool or club for that shot.

Most amateur golfers spend way too much time trying not to hit bad shots rather than focussing their attention on creating good shots. You always have a choice. Choose wisely.

The Very Real Power Of Imagination

Imagination / ɪˌmadʒɪˈneɪʃ(ə)n / noun. The ability of the mind to be creative or resourceful

In the process of writing this book, we combined our own personal experiences with scientific research to back up our belief that golf is largely a creative art.

In our quest to provide you with the best possible information, we found a fascinating piece of research conducted by a team from the University of Boulder Colorado.

According to Tor Wagner, director of the Cognitive and Affective Neuroscience Laboratory at CU Boulder, and co-author of the paper which was published in the journal Neuron: "This research confirms that imagination is a neurological reality that can impact our brains and bodies in ways that matter for our wellbeing."

The researchers measured brain activity using magnetic resonance imaging (MRI). Sensors on the skin measured how the body responded. You might be wondering how this applies to golf. Think about it in terms of some of the disappointing golf shots you may have hit.

According to the lead author of the paper, Marianne Cumella Reddan: "If you have a memory that is no longer useful for you or is crippling you, you can use imagination to tap into it, change it and re-consolidate it, updating the way you think about and experience something." As imagination becomes a more common tool among clinicians, the team at CU Boulder believes more research is apparently necessary.

However, for now, advises Wagner: "Pay attention to what you imagine. Manage your imagination and what you permit yourself to imagine. You can use imagination constructively to shape what your brain learns from experience."

You have probably read numerous magazine articles and watched countless YouTube videos telling you to see the shot before you execute it but that isn't always as easy as it sounds.

So how can we make it easier for you? If we were to ask you what your car looks like, or what your next-door neighbour's dog looks like, this would trigger something in your mind.

In all probability, you would see a pretty vivid image of exactly what your car or next-door neighbour's dog looks like. You can probably even hear the dog bark. That is a prime example of using your imagination.

Why does this work? We go back to one of the fundamentals of this book: Asking good questions.

Questions focus the mind and provide you with a single point of focused attention.

'Single point' is a technique that has been used very successfully by martial-arts practitioners for centuries and we have seen, first hand, the benefits of using that single point of focused attention when it comes to creating shots on the golf course.

Ask yourself good questions and you will come up with good answers. Answers that are as unique as you and your golf swing are.

We could ask 10 players what a good shot looks like from 165 yards to a flag in the back-right portion of the green and we might get a variety of answers. Some will see a high shot fading towards the flag, others might see a draw starting at the flag and flying towards the middle of the green, and some might see a dead straight bullet going straight at it. Some might see it flying high, others may see it coming in on a lower trajectory.

Which one is correct? It could well be that they all are, depending on the individual.

If you are more comfortable moving the ball left to right than right to left, then a fade is more than likely to be your best option.

If you have a very clear picture of what that shot looks like and believe you can create it, then that is the correct option for you.

Remember our old friends the thinker and the prover? What the thinker thinks, the prover proves.

Watching golf on TV has become so much more enjoyable and insightful since the introduction of the shot tracker and associated graphics. So much so that when we see a shot without it, we are often more than a little disappointed. We can see the shot in its entirety, from launch to landing and everything in between. The height, arc and shape. High, low, draw, fade or relatively straight.

One thing that fascinated and dare I say surprised us when we started to look at the ball flight graphics when using TrackMan is that while most golfers tend to see draw or fade as a continuous curve, that isn't actually the case.

What actually happens is that when the speed or velocity of the ball decreases, so does the amount of spin. As we said before, the ball spinning on a tilted axis is what gives the illusion of sidespin and curvature of the shot. As the velocity and spin are reduced, therefore so is the amount of shape on the ball.

When Tiger Woods first saw and understood this, it totally changed how much shape he saw when visualising fades and draws.

He said: "It really helped me to see my shots much more clearly. I started to understand that I could actually aim within the parameters of the fairway to hit fades and draws and still find the fairway. Whereas before I was starting my fades and draws over the rough, water or bunkers beyond the confines of the fairway."

Often TV commentators are fooled when they see a ball 'hooking' that looks like it is going to miss the green left, only to see it straighten out towards the end of its flight as the speed and spin of the ball diminishes and land on the edge of the green rather than the greenside bunker.

Launch monitors have many uses but we doubt many golfers or coaches are using them as a shot-visualisation tool. When we are working with a player on what a good shot looks like, using the graphic of a good shot they have hit is an incredibly powerful tool.

Not only does it allow them to get a crystal-clear picture of what a good shot looks like with a particular club, it lets them see a great example of a good shot that they have created.

Armed with that visual and the knowledge they can indeed create great golf shots, they are far more confident and comfortable with the task of visualising and creating the next one.

We are used to seeing the shot tracker on our TV screens from behind the player – or 'down the line'.

As helpful as that may be, if you use your own version of that to help you to visualise the shot you want to create or invent, it doesn't tell the full story. While it tracks the ball beautifully and accurately through the air, this view doesn't tell us what happens when the ball hits the ground.

As we all know, a golf ball rarely comes to an abrupt halt as soon as it hits the deck. Depending on the ground conditions – wet and soft, dry and firm, whether it lands on a flat piece of ground or kicks off a slope – the ball will react differently.

This has to be taken into consideration when you visualise and play any shot on any hole on any given day. Will the ball bounce, stop, move to the left or right or go straight ahead?

This part of the shot is often omitted or neglected in the visualisation process but is definitely something that needs to be factored in. You must be aware of what that shot looks like, in its entirety, from start to finish, if you are to create that shot successfully.

Imagine if you could see that shot from both down the line and side on. Down the line will help you see where your ball starts, the apex and curvature and where it lands.

Looking at it from side on allows you to see the shot like a rainbow with the added advantage of how the ball reacts when it hits the ground.

Think about your shots on and around the greens. When you visualise a putt, hopefully you will see the ball falling into the hole and not pulling up an inch or two short. When you play a pitch shot or a chip and run, you will more than likely have a spot in your mind's eye where you want the ball to land and hopefully you will see how your ball is going to react on the green.

You will hopefully be reading these shots in the same way as you read a putt. You will be seeing the ball from the start of its journey until it reaches its final destination.

You are also learning the art and skill of prediction as a by-product. You are learning how to predict how the ball will react from when it comes off the clubface to the end of its journey.

If you can't or don't see the entire journey of the ball, it is akin to not putting a postcode or zip code into your sat-nav. If you only type in the town or city and not the postcode, you will end up somewhere in that town or city but it is highly unlikely that you will end up at your desired destination.

Make sure you give all your shots a postcode. Is it possible that you can hit a great shot, chip, pitch or putt? Absolutely.

What does the ball need to do to achieve that?

These are great questions that will help you to come up with equally great visuals, solutions and ultimately great shots.

You often hear stories of top tour pros rediscovering their form as a result of watching old footage of when they were playing their best. Watching these videos tends to reignite positive memories of what their good shots looked like and perhaps what they were thinking or working on at the time.

Now, unless you are a tour pro, it's unlikely you will be able to find footage of your previous golfing exploits on the internet. Not too many monthly medals are beamed live into the homes of golf fans around the world.

However, if your coach has a launch monitor, the chances are that he or she will be able to go into your shot library and find some footage of your best shots. We didn't say your best swings but your best shots.

Ask to have a look. Ask to see evidence of the good shots you know you have and can hit.

Watch the fight of the ball. Did it match up it your expectations? Did it match up to the visualisation you created in your mind? Do you remember what that shot felt like as it left the clubface? Do you remember how you reacted to it? Did it make you smile? Did you enjoy the experience and the moment? If the answer to these questions is a resounding yes then it is indeed possible that you can create good shots.

You are looking at the evidence rather than relying on your own or someone else's opinion.

To create a shot that looks and feels exactly as you had envisioned and hoped it would is incredibly satisfying and rewarding. Your reactions and associated feelings release a chemical called serotonin, which has a wide variety of functions in the human body.

It is sometimes called the happy chemical because it contributes to wellbeing and happiness. The more good shots you hit, the more serotonin flows through your body. The more this happens, the more you crave it. Perhaps that is why creating good shots and playing your best golf can make it almost addictive.

In the interests of speed of play (which as we all know is a concern) and creating better shots, the sooner you react to the mental image or images of the shot you see, the easier it will be to create that shot. The longer you stand over the ball, the more then image you have created in your mind's eye will fade.

Over and above that, your attention may well drift towards your backswing, your score or some other unhelpful distraction.

In short, once you have asked and answered the questions, see the shot, feel the shot, create the shot and, most importantly of all, enjoy the shot.

Training Exercises

Too often we see golfers of all standards using the course as a proving ground rather than a training ground. As soon as you step on to the 1st tee or put a scorecard in your pocket, you start to think about what kind of score you are going to shoot. Thoughts of scores relative to par or your handicap start to fill your mind. The desire to prove to yourself and others that you are capable of shooting a good score becomes all-consuming.

However, if you ask most good golfers where they learned to play, they will tell you it was on a course. They may well have honed certain skills on the driving range but the golf course is where they actually learned to play. With that in mind, don't be afraid to use the course as a learning and training ground. We know this might go against popular opinion, but let's think about playing to learn rather than learning to play.

Forget about your score, handicap or par once in a while and take the opportunity to put your newly acquired visualisation skills to good use on the golf course. After all, that is where you are going to use and apply them going forwards if you are to make any real progress. Yes, you can use the following exercises on the range with a bit of imagination and we would encourage you to do so but please don't limit them to the range. You cannot learn the skill of getting up and down to save par or make birdie on the driving range.

We are very aware that pace of play is a concern so we would encourage you to train all your skills both on the range and the course, so they become second nature. As the quality of your training improves, so will your performance.

Asking quality questions will provide quality answers and, as a direct result, your decision-making process will become more efficient and effective.

1 Visualise A Wider Channel

One of the many things we have learned from the feedback we frequently receive from our book The Lost Art Of Putting is that when we give players a wider channel or thicker line to hit the ball down, there are benefits to be found on many different levels.

When putting, the vast majority of players tend to see a very thin line to the hole. This, in turn, creates tension and thoughts of 'don't let the ball fall off that line'. As a direct result, that prevents or inhibits any kind of free-flowing motion in the putting stroke.

The same can be said when we visualise a very thin line for full shots. Think for a moment about how wide your internal shot tracker looks. Chances are, it's not even as wide as the golf ball. If you are trying to get your golf ball to travel on a trajectory line that is less than 1.68 inches wide, you are going to struggle.

Visualising a thin line or a very small point in the distance may well work for you and if that is the case, please continue to do so.

If, however, it isn't working for you, by giving yourself a wider line or channel to hit your ball down, the likelihood is that your body and mind will be freed up, allowing you to make a more relaxed and committed swing.

Experiment a little with width of channel. See what kind of shots you create when you have a five, 10 or 15-yard channel to play down. If your good shots had a colour, what colour would they be? Colour in the channel or corridor you are going to play down. It might be red, yellow, blue, white or orange.

Experiment with different widths and colours until you find a combination that works for you. Have some fun with it in the process. We talked about visualisation creating a neural pathway; now we can add to this by creating a virtual pathway in the form of a wider, brightly coloured channel.

Regardless of how narrow the fairway or green is, the chances are it won't be less than five, 10 or 15 yards.

As we often say to our students, although a fairway or green may look relatively small or narrow, there is more than enough room for your golf ball.

2 The Three-Lane Highway
Once you have asked the questions 'what is the shot', 'is it possible

I can create this shot' and 'what does a good shot look like', experiment with this as a concept.

Imagine the fairway or green you are looking to hit is a three-lane highway. You can colour-code the lanes to help create real definition – left-hand lane yellow, middle-lane red and right-hand lane blue or whatever suits you.

If you are clear in your mind that the best, most reliable, option for you is a fade, for example, visualise your ball starting in the left-hand lane and fading back towards the middle lane.

If the shot you see and are comfortable with is a draw, picture it starting in the right-hand lane and drawing back towards the middle lane. If you see a dead-straight bullet, fire it straight down that middle lane. Remember to factor in how your prediction of how the ball will react once it lands on the green or fairway as this is a vital part of the shot.

Make sure you don't leave the cinema during the final scene or you will never know how your movie ends.

3 Make Short Game Practice Real

When we speak to our students about the concepts of 'we create what we see' and visualisation, we explain the benefits and help them find their way of applying and implementing the process. Then we see some real breakthroughs – light-bulb moments. Not only when it comes to full shots but also in the short game, perhaps even more so.

Assuming you set aside time to work on your short game, what does your current short-game practice or training regime look like?

Do you take a load of golf balls and practise the same shot from the same spot in the hope you will improve through repetition?

Thought so. But do you get a second, third, fourth and fifth chance on the course? No. So why practise that way?

If you practise this way, you will ultimately become good at one thing: namely practising this way.

Just as you would on the course, play one shot at a time. Just as you would on the course, ask yourself good questions: What is the shot?

Is it possible I could hit a great shot here? Is it possible this could be the best chip, pitch or bunker shot I have ever hit in my life? What does the ball need to do? What does a good shot look like?

Only then, once you have a very clear intention and image of what that shot looks and feels like, should you select the best club for the task at hand and create that shot.

Vary your shots. Vary the clubs you use to create these shots. One at a time. Explore what is possible.

Not only will you find out what works best for you, this journey of discovery will be a fun, educational and rewarding experience which will stand you in good stead for when you next face these shots on the course.

The Impact Of Launch Monitors

Since the widespread use of launch monitors over the last 10 years or so, the way we look at and play the game has changed dramatically and changed for the better.

Rather than guessing why the ball has behaved in a particular manner on any given shot, we now know the root cause thanks to doppler radar technology that accurately measures not only what the ball does in flight but what the golf club is doing at impact. As our good friends at TrackMan, the industry leaders in club and ball tracking data, say: "Why guess what you can measure?"

Most of the world's best players trust TrackMan to help them in their quest to become the best they can possibly be. Endorsements don't come much stronger than that.

For those of us who grew up learning the 'old' ball flight laws taught by PGAs around the world, we now know that their information was pretty much entirely inaccurate and incorrect.

Thankfully, as a result of data collected from hundreds of thousands of shots hit, we now know that, essentially, wherever the clubface is pointing at the moment of maximum compression (which TrackMan use as their data collection point) will largely influence the launch direction of the shot.

We also know that the swing path will largely influence the curvature of the shot.

In essence the face sends it and the path bends it, assuming a centred strike. We say assuming a centred strike because there are other factors which can influence the curvature of any shot – such as off-centred strikes which in turn create gear effect.

If you are keen to learn more about the influence of off-centred strikes and gear effect have on golf shots, we strongly recommend you visit trackmangolf.com, where you will find some fantastic information to help you gain a clear understanding of what really happens when you miss the sweet spot.

We are very fortunate to have developed an exceptional working relationship with TrackMan over the years and the data they provide us with through their technology on a daily basis is invaluable.

Ultimately, TrackMan is an incredibly accurate measuring device and over and above using their graphics to show what a good shot looks like, it should be used as such.

One of the many things we love about it is that is does not and cannot form an opinion. The golf industry is awash with opinions, most of which are conflicting, confusing and largely unhelpful.

We often refer to TrackMan as the truth serum. It will not form an opinion. It will, however, provide you with facts. Only a fool, surely, would argue with factual data.

Beyond simply gathering club and ball data when a player is hitting balls on the range, we use TrackMan for measuring what happens depending on where a player places their attention. What started out as a bit of an experiment has become massively influential and helpful in our coaching.

In order to discover what works best for a certain player, we ask them to hit a few shots with their attention on a variety of different things. For example, we might ask a player to hit a couple of shots with their focussed attention on their backswing. We may then ask them to hit a couple of shots with their attention on the clubhead. Perhaps a couple of shots focussing on whatever they are currently working on, which can be weird, wonderful and varied.

Incidentally, some of the things we hear that people are working on are beyond belief or comprehension – often on the recommendation of one of their Saturday morning playing partners who is an expert because he once hit a drive 270 yards. The mind boggles.

The reason we ask players to hit shots with their attention on different things is to allow us to discover where their attention works best for them. After all, the most important thing in golf is what we do with the golf ball. Sadly in coaching, this is largely and inexplicably overlooked.

Some players produce their best results when they have an internal focus – ie: a body part or a backswing thought. But they are very much in the minority from our own findings and those of others whose research we believe in and respect.

Others perform best when they have an external focus, where their attention on what the clubhead is doing for example.

However, our own personal findings suggest that the vast majority of players have the greatest success and control of their golf ball when they are paying attention to what the ball has to do in order to reach its intended target.

Hence the importance of the question: What does a good shot look like?

When a player becomes absorbed and engaged in the creation of a shot having asked that incredibly simple and powerful question, their ability to create that shot is quite staggering.

We create what we see. If you can't see it, good luck creating it.

Using the shot tracker graphic to show a player what a good shot looks like, quite literally unlocks their mind, takes the brakes off their thoughts and swing and allows them to create the shot they see. Wouldn't it be great if you could watch or play golf with the shot tracker showing you the shot before you hit it? The benefits would be immense. It would create a crystal-clear image of the shot you want to create and provide a pathway in your mind's eye for your ball to follow.

While you may not be able physically to do this, you can certainly use the imagery from shots stored on TrackMan to create a visual library in your mind.

Using the data collected by TrackMan, we can also help a player to gain a clear understanding of what a particular shot feels like when their attention is in a certain place.

When players hit their best shots, we always encourage them to describe what that shot felt like and ask if it matched up to the image they have formed in their mind. This process is extremely helpful and rewarding for the player as it provides confirmation that having a single point of focused attention allows them to create the shot they desire. Again, that is not our opinion, we have accurate data to back it up.

The vast majority of top club fitters, coaches and players around the world trust TrackMan, so why wouldn't we?

Once you understand what a good shot looks and feels like and you have data to back it up, ask your TrackMan operator to send you a screencast reminding you of where your attention was and what happened to the ball as a direct result. You can then view this on your smartphone, tablet or laptop and refer to it when you go to the range or before you head out on to the course.

All too often, golfers tend to pay their coach a visit when they are playing badly to get a quick fix. We know this doesn't work. It's like putting a band-aid on an open wound.

The best time to see your coach is when you are playing well so that you can understand why.

If you are going to use TrackMan to help you with your game, and we strongly recommend you do, please make sure that the operator is suitably trained and qualified.

TrackMan have a fantastic online education programme – TrackMan University – where there is an abundance of excellent information, which is both easy to understand and apply.

We have heard some ridiculous accusations that TrackMan ruined a certain player but that is absolute nonsense. As we said before, it does not have an opinion. TrackMan has never ruined anyone: the operator and his opinions might but not the device itself.

Find a coach or pro who has the appropriate knowledge and experience and knows the numbers inside out, preferably a

TrackMan Master. You will be able to find one via the TrackMan Locator on their website. A smart coach will keep the amount of data you are exposed to down to a minimum in order to provide you with clarity, not clutter.

We often refer to our coaching sessions as a time for a mental de-clutter, stripping back all the surplus information, leaving you to focus your attention on what is truly useful. TrackMan is an essential tool in helping us to do just that. That is the strongest endorsement we can offer and we thank the team at TrackMan for their continued innovation and support.

Key Takeaways

1 Before you hit any shot it is essential that you have a very clear picture of what the very best version of that shot looks like.

2 Most amateur golfers spend way too much time trying not to hit bad shots rather than focussing their attention on creating good shots.

3 See the shot, feel the shot, create the shot and, most importantly of all, enjoy the shot.

4 Don't be afraid to use the course as a learning and training ground. Think about playing to learn rather than learning to play.

5 Thanks to launch monitors like TrackMan we now know that, in essence, the face sends it and the path bends it – assuming a centred strike.

Chapter 5
WHAT IS YOUR STRATEGY FOR PLAYING GOLF?

Strategy begins long before you reach the 1st tee. And it doesn't end until after the final putt is holed

Strategy / ˈstratɪdʒi / Noun. **A plan of action designed to achieve a long-term or overall aim.**

DO you have a strategy for how you are going to play the golf course? By strategy, we mean have you ever actually sat down and thought about the best way for you to shoot your best, stress-free score?

Or, do you do what most golfers do and hit driver as hard as you can on every par 4 and 5 and see what happens after that?

If you do have a strategy, where and when does it start? Does your strategy include how you are going to prepare both mentally and physically or do you generally just wait until you get to the 1st tee?

What you do before you head to the 1st tee can and will influence your attitude and performance on the golf course.

A bad attitude is like a flat tyre: You can't go anywhere until you change it.

How many times have you gone out on the course without hitting any shots on the range to warm up beforehand only to play terribly for the first few holes before you find your game?

Essentially, you are using the first few holes as warm-up holes, by which time you have run up a couple of double bogeys, duffed a couple of chips and three-putted twice. Score ruined. We've all been there but this scenario can be avoided if you prepare properly.

As Benjamin Franklin famously said: "By failing to prepare, you are preparing to fail."

The Importance Of Preparation

Preparation / ˌprɛpəˈreɪʃ(ə)n / Noun. The things that you do or the time that you spend preparing for something.

There are hundreds of inspirational quotes on preparation but we have chosen a few that we believe you will find pertinent:

"Success is where preparation and opportunity meet."
– Bobby Unser

"Proper preparation prevents poor performance."
– Stephen Keague

"Before anything else, preparation is the key to success."
– Alexander Graham Bell

"Success depends upon previous preparation and without such preparation, there is sure to be failure."
– Confucius

"The meeting of preparation with opportunity generates the offspring we call luck."
– Tony Robbins

While there may not be one singular magic formula for success or preparation, we do believe there are a number of methods you can explore to discover your best way to prepare. For most weekend golfers, preparation is getting to the golf club just in time to tee off. However, if you want to get the most out of yourself and your time on the course, you might want to look into some of the following ideas.

Golf is very much a game of attention. The golf course demands that your attention is in the right place at the right time. But do you ever train your attention? Thought not.

We will share a couple of attention exercises but, in the meantime, please understand that training your attention is not to be underestimated. Pre-round preparation is not just walking onto the range and smashing a few drivers then putting with three balls for five minutes before rushing to the 1st tee.

Preparation starts with having a plan of action, a clear intention. Only when you have a crystal-clear intention do you have somewhere to place your attention.

We've walked hundreds of practice and tournament rounds with tour pros over the years, and we've learned that while each individual player may well have their own masterplan as to how the are going to pick the course apart, their end goal is always the same.

Their aim is to put together a plan to give themselves the best possible opportunity to shoot their best possible score and that is exactly what they are paying attention to during their practice rounds.

With that in mind, we are not going to suggest you hit irons off every tee for position or safety. Especially if your driver is the best club in your bag.

In all probability, you will shoot lower scores if your approach shots are played with a wedge or 9-iron in your hand rather than a hybrid or a 4-iron.

We are however, going to suggest a suitable and applicable strategy based on our observations and learnings from watching and discussing with golfers who make their living from the game.

Club golfers the world over spend a disproportionate amount of time focussing on how they are going to hit their ball compared to where they are going to hit it. Perhaps more importantly, they spend even less time thinking about why they are going to try to hit it to a certain spot on the fairway or green.

Successful tournament professionals, on the other hand, pay a lot of attention to where and why they are going to hit their shots, not just how.

If you look at the yardage books that these guys use, you will see there is an incredible amount of detail. Distances to and over certain fairway bunkers and water hazards.

How far it is before they run out of fairway. How long the green is from front to back. Where the slopes are on the greens.

No laser or GPS device, as good as they are, can yet tell you how much green you have behind the flag or where the slopes on the greens are.

Tour yardage books are incredibly detailed and enable players to make informed decisions. No guesswork here.

We understand that not everywhere you play will have an amazing course guide or planner.

If they don't, why not make one of your own? It is an incredibly insightful experience and something you may want to consider. You will discover some subtle nuances about your home course that you were previously unaware of.

You may think because you have played a certain course dozens of times that you know every blade of grass and grain of sand like the back of your hand. The chances are that there are many aspects you have never even noticed.

If you are walking around with your head down, cursing your luck about that bad break you had on the previous hole when your ball bounced into the greenside bunker, you will see very little other than the fact your shoes could probably do with a clean.

Elsewhere in this book we have talked about the benefits of walking with your eyes above the level of the flag.

When it comes to working out a strategy, this concept can really make a massive difference. If you're not looking, you're not learning. We also talked about the course designer effectively being your opponent. A good golf course designer or architect is constantly asking interesting and pertinent questions of you the golfer.

If your eyes are checking out nothing more than the grass beneath your feet and your shoes, your ability to answer these questions is limited at best.

Does the golf course, hole or even the shot you are about to face inspire confidence or fear? Either way, your confidence will be directly affected.

If you are looking down a nice wide fairway with a generous landing area and very little in the way of risk, the likelihood is you will think 'I can really relax and let one rip down here' as you reach for your driver, confident in your ability to hit the fairway.

Conversely, if you are looking down a narrow tree-lined fairway with bunkers in the landing area, your head might start to fill with different thoughts.

We talk elsewhere in some detail about the power of visualisation and using your imagination out on the golf course.

However, you don't need to wait until you get to the 1st tee before you start employing your imagination and visualisation skills. For decades, sportsmen and women have been using these skills before they play. Formula 1 drivers are well known for visualising the race track and how they are going to get round it as quickly as possible.

They know exactly how fast they can take a certain corner and what gear they need to select in order to hit the apex of the corner or find the racing line. Michael Schumacher, one of Formula 1's most prolific champions, believed this gave him a massive advantage.

Over and above being extremely aware and well prepared for the race ahead, he believed he was in full race mode by the time he got to the starting grid. In his mind he was already three or four laps into the race, whereas his competitors were still focussed on making a decent start.

Skiers picture the downhill or slalom course they are about to face. These crazy bobsleigh riders, whose objective of hurtling down a solid ice track in a fibreglass tube on four blades as fast as they possibly can without crashing, wouldn't dream of setting off unless they had a very clear picture in their minds of where all the twists and turns were and how they were going to negotiate them.

Not only does visualisation and crystal-clear imagery help you prepare for what you are about to face, whatever that may be, it actually puts you into playing mode.

We encourage the golfers we work with to use these skills as part of their warm-up on the range.

To imagine and create the shots they are likely to face on the course. To have fun shaping the ball in different ways. To hit high shots and low ones.

One of our favourite warm-up and preparation exercises is to play nine or even 18 holes on the range before you go out to play. This has many benefits on many different levels. By playing golf on the range, hitting shots a specific distance in a specific direction to specific targets, you are training and preparing for what you have to do on the golf course.

All too often we hear of golfers who struggle to take their range game to the course, largely because their practice and preparation don't even closely resemble golf.

Let's face it, unless the range you use has clearly defined fairways, greens and distance markers, you are pretty much hitting balls into a wide open space, unconsciously aiming at nothing in particular.

As the legendary coach Butch Harmon once said: "If you aim at nothing, you'll hit it every time."

Butch has had a massive influence on coaching over the years and is a great believer in getting the basics right – like grip, posture and alignment to your intended target – all of which are often overlooked in both preparation and play. If you don't keep an eye on them in your practice or training, you are unlikely even to be aware of them on the course.

However, get the basics right in your training and these fundamentals will stand you in good stead when you play. The better you prepare, the better your chances of performing where and when it matters.

Justin Rose has come an awful long way since missing his first 21 cuts as a tournament professional. He's won around the world, including the 2013 US Open and the gold medal at the 2016 Olympic Games in Rio de Janeiro.

He puts an incredible amount of faith and belief in preparation.

"Preparation quietens the mind," he says. "It might not guarantee anything but when you get to the 1st tee safe in the knowledge you have done everything you can to prepare, it then simply becomes a case of being in the moment and playing golf one shot at a time."

Transferability has become a buzzword in sports in general and golf in particular and the closer your training and preparation are to actually playing golf, the easier it will be transfer your range game onto the course.

Most golfers, at all levels, including professionals with years of experience, tend to do 'block' practice.

They start their practice session by hitting 10 balls with their most lofted wedge, followed by 10 balls with their pitching wedge, then 10 balls with a 9- iron, 8-iron, 7-iron, all the way through the bag, finishing with 10 full blooded drivers.

Think about this for a second or two. At what level does this make any sense? If you go through this process, all you will have really learned or experienced is that you have the ability to hit ball after ball with every club in your bag in a structured sequence. Does that sound like playing golf?

In our best-selling book The Lost Art Of Putting, we talk about the importance of practising or training using one ball. Not two, not three but one.

If you have three balls to putt with from the same spot to the same hole, how much attention are you really paying to the first ball, knowing you have another one or two attempts? Not a whole lot.

The same principle applies when you go to the range or the practice ground. We are not suggesting you go to the range with one ball but we are saying that you should only ever be paying attention to one shot at a time.

After all, we can only play one shot at a time but all too often we see golfers prepare for their round by hitting ball after ball with the same club to the same target. The very thought of doing that sounds so boring, it's little wonder so many golfers find practice both mind-numbingly dull and ineffective.

This kind of practice is not training or preparing for what you are about to encounter on the golf course.

Do you ever practise or train hitting shots from the rough? Do you ever practise your pitching or chipping from tight lies around the green or from bad lies in a bunker? If not, you will never be able to predict how the ball is going to react.

Until you work on playing different shots from different lies in different conditions, the skill or art of predicting how your ball will react will elude you.

For many golfers, the word strategy is limited to how they are going to play a particular tee shot on a particular hole and with what club. This is obviously a consideration but don't limit yourself to physical strategies.

The 2018 Open champion, Francesco Molinari, who became the first European player ever to win five points out of five in the Ryder Cup, made a very interesting comment after winning the 2019 Arnold Palmer Invitational at Bay Hill.

Italy's most successful golfer said: "My strategy was to keep hitting good shots."

Note how he didn't say anything about making good swings. His intention was to keep hitting good shots and therefore his attention and focus was directed to doing just that. The record books will show that he shot an incredible bogey-free eight-under-par 64 in the final round to win by two shots.

In his post-round interview he said it was 'probably my best putting round ever' but in order to set up those birdie putts he had to be hitting good shots.

While this may seem like a pretty simple strategy or philosophy, it is clearly one that works for him. Francesco is a smart guy and an extremely hard working and talented golfer who loves simplicity in many forms when it comes to golf.

In an instruction article in Today's Golfer magazine, he said: "I like simple swing thoughts and ideas."

Throughout the article, he talks an awful lot of sense and perhaps we could all learn something from his thoughts.

"When you are on the range before you play, look carefully at what the ball is doing," he said. "You'll most likely find that one predominant shot shape comes easily to you on the day. That's just how golf is. Instead of trying to fight it, like a lot of players do, just go with it and use it to your advantage off the tee and into the greens." Pretty straightforward stuff, we are sure you will agree.

He continued: "For the average golfer, the secret to hitting more greens is picking a club that should easily find the safety of the middle of the green. You shouldn't always just go for the flags because, very often, in doing so, you can end up in all kinds of trouble.

"Always play to the distance of the middle of the green. Percentage-wise it's more simple and is likely to give you a better scoring chance than going for a short flag and coming up short or going for a back flag and flying the green."

Perhaps Francesco's best piece of advice was also the simplest when he said: "My personal swing thought is to focus on hitting the ball in the middle of the clubface. It really is as simple as that. No complex swing plane or takeaway thoughts. If you can get clean contact every time, you get more consistency in shape and distance control. Even half-decent contact on the ball will rule out a disaster scenario." Wise words indeed.

Looking From A Different Perspective

A question we often ask the players we work with is: 'Who is your opponent?' Often the reply will come back as 'myself', often with a tone of amusement stemming from a premise that we have never heard that phrase before. We have and it is the wrong answer.

The next answer is then often 'the golf course' and while that is close it is still incorrect.

For us, your opponent when you play golf is the course designer.

The person who designed the golf course you are about to play did not design it so you could just go out and make lots of pars and birdies and never lose a ball otherwise you would just play a wide-open field with no hazards.

A great golf course designer wants to test your ability to play golf shots.

The central theme of this book, the ability to play golf shots, is also central to a course designer's thinking.

They don't mind if you make some pars and birdies but you have to earn the right to put these numbers on your scorecard.

The really effective course designer has the ability to create some strong visual effects.

As you stand on the tee and you look down the fairway and you feel your tension levels increase a little as you see this hole as being a tough challenge then the course designer is already winning the battle not to relinquish a par or a birdie.

If you stand in the middle of the fairway and you feel that the approach into the green is less than straightforward then again the 'picture' of the hole provided to you is doing its job of increasing the sense of difficulty and challenge.

Yet when you start to look at the game through the lens we have suggested a new world opens up.

If you see the game in terms of creating golf shots you then get to drill even deeper and start to be able to put a plan together of how to beat your opponent – the course designer.

You start to love the opportunity to study a golf hole and come up with a way that you as an individual can give that very course designer a run for their money.

One way you can get really good at this is that course designers create many optical illusions of reality.

For example, if you stand on a narrow tee it can create a perception of a narrower fairway than is actually the case.

Perhaps the greatest mind that has ever competed in the game of golf was that of Jack Nicklaus.

He used to walk golf courses backwards.

To the both of us, this makes absolutely perfect sense.

Our suggestion would be that first of all you look at the golf course you play most regularly, starting at the back of the 18th green.

As you stand at the back of a green we guarantee as you look at that green and then scan the fairway for the best approach you will see the hole in a totally different light.

You raise the curtain and reveal some of the illusions your course designer has employed to make you approach the green with trepidation. You will be stunned as you look at the course from a different perspective.

Think about what we normally do habitually. We play a hole and knock the final putt in and then bury our heads as we stalk off to the next tee. We almost never take the time to really look at the structure of the hole from the back of the green.

From this perspective the intention of the designer is laid bare and you can see the opportunities of how you can best approach the green and then what the green demands of you when you get there.

When you become fascinated at the way golf courses are laid out and the way that you can design your shots to defeat the course designer, you then genuinely embrace the art of playing golf.

You will probably find as you look from the back of the green you will start to visualise the potential shots you can hit in. You will be stretching your imagination muscles.

The very same principle applies as you walk backwards all the way up the hole.

You will again see how the course designer has used the contours of the land to make a hole look challenging.

Of course, many holes are genuinely challenging and do require you to hit quality shots but with this training approach you will start to see so many more options.

Do the exercise all the way up to the tee – look backwards and look forwards.

Start to put together your own strategy.

Once you play a hole and you execute the plan you first created in your mind you will feel a leap of enthusiasm as you walk off the hole in the knowledge that on this particular occasion you have taken on the course designer and in your own way given him a run for his money.

Getting The Job Done

So much of the art of playing golf is about being able to deal with the inevitable chaos the game throws at you.

The skill of adaptability is supreme.

This means instead of having a mindset of delusional hope that everything will somehow be perfect with your game today you develop the ability to know yourself and what you have on the unique day that is today.

If you had your game totally under control, you could hit it high, low or neutral. You would be able to hit a draw, a fade or a straight shot. How wonderful would that be?

Unfortunately, this is probably never going to happen, even for the very, very best in the world apart from on a few rare days for a tiny minority of the elite.

Total ball control is a lovely concept but the idea runs up against an impractical reality of golfing unpredictability.

However, the good news is you only need one of those shapes of shot and you are in business.

If, when you warm up, the only shot you have is a high fade then you can still play wonderfully effective golf if you make your decisions on the course based around that reality. You create shots with the capability you have today.

Jack Nicklaus used to say: "You have to dance with the lady that brought you."

To go with the game you have today instead of taking on shots you have no chance of executing.

This takes a lot of mental discipline but is ultimately very rewarding when you manage your game so well that you get the ball around the course in a decent score when you are far from being your best.

Please understand, we are not saying you should be satisfied long-term with what you have today.

This entire book is encouraging you to develop your game and the shots you can play. What we are saying is that it takes a supremely effective thinker to play today with the tools you have in the bag.

If that means you lay up instead of leaving the 50-yard pitch you are struggling with then so be it. If it means hitting a 3-wood fade off the tee to find the fairway on a long, right-to-left dogleg then you have out-thought the course designer with what you have today.

At times, it may not be pretty – but it can be wonderfully effective.

Once you get out on the course the game will always throw lots of curve balls at you. It is all going great one minute then a run of poor shots appears from nowhere.

So we want to introduce you to the concept of Reset.

Reset is the ability to get your precious attention back to the here and now to get the job done.

When things are going wrong, it is so easy to fall into a pit of mental despair. Our attention ends up being anywhere other than the place it needs to be as we create all kinds of doomsday scenarios in our mind.

In many ways the 'goal' of 18 holes is far too big.

It's too big a chunk to chew.

There is too much variability. Four hours of unpredictability to build a score can be very difficult from a mental game perspective.

So we are going to suggest you stop trying to play golf as a 18-hole challenge and embrace the concept of 'Super 6'.

The game becomes simply six sets of three holes.

Your task is to play each set of three to the best of your ability then after every set you reset.

You bring your attention back to the here and now and you have a new game to play.

Just this set of three. Mark the sets of three on your card.

After every three holes go through a physical ritual such as taking a drink as a way to section the threes.

We have found this is a wonderful way of leaving behind what has happened and being able to re-focus on what is here right now.

And it's a concept that works both for good and bad days.

If you have had a poor start then it is great to reset on the 4th tee. You begin again and the human mind loves the concept of a fresh start or a new beginning.

Just think how we embrace the possibility of a new year with our resolutions as we aim to shake off the limiting patterns and habits of the previous year.

If you are doing well, then instead of protecting your score and trying to hold on you simply reset and focus on the next set of three. A new challenge, a new start.

It is deceptively simple but profoundly effective.

If you are really struggling then remember the theme we have talked so much about, both in this book and The Lost Art of Putting – namely the value of questions.

When your back is to the wall and you have racked up some high numbers, or indeed if you have the potential to shoot the lights out, it is so easy for our mind to do time travel and create all kinds of potential outcomes and scenarios.

When this is happening you can really ground yourself in the present by asking the simple question: What is the task?

Right here and now: What is the task?

Simply to move this ball here to that target over there.

Anything else is just noise.

This simple little question has the power to bring you back to the only thing you have any control over – which is what you decide to focus on with this shot right here and now.

That single question will allow you to get the job done on a more regular basis. It won't stop the chaos that is golf but it does give you a laser-like tool to deal with that chaos.

How Do You Deal With Pressure?

We are often asked the question: "How do I deal with pressure on the course?"

First and foremost, we believe you need to understand what pressure is and where it comes from.

Pressure occurs when you find yourself in a situation that makes you feel somewhat uneasy. While it might not feel like it at the time, this is where you can actually learn an awful lot. We tend not to learn a whole lot in our comfort zone where we feel happy and at ease.

Stepping out of your comfort zone and embracing the situation provides you with an incredible learning opportunity – one that you can take with you and draw upon in the future.

Where does pressure come from? It comes from within. Always. Pressure is essentially when you allow your attention to shift from the task at hand to the potential or perceived consequences of your actions.

Do golf swings and putting strokes change under pressure? Yes, they can do but while the situation itself doesn't cause that change, the importance you place on the outcome of the tournament, round or shot you are faced with almost certainly does.

Everyone who has ever played this great game will have stood on the 1st tee and experienced a sense of anxiety, anticipation and nervousness. That is entirely normal, entirely human.

What causes these emotions to come to the fore? The reasons are varied and numerous but ultimately it boils down to the fact that you have allowed your attention to wander.

The thoughts that run through our minds go from 'just make contact' to 'don't make a fool of yourself' to 'don't hit it out of bounds!' We are terrified that people watching are going to judge us and think less of us if we don't hit a perfect tee shot that splits the middle of the fairway.

Sound familiar? Of course it does. The good news is that these emotions make you feel alive. They make you aware that something special could happen. Rather than thinking of 1st tee nerves, rephrase and reframe this experience as 1st tee energy and adrenaline – something that you can use to your advantage.

Your initial thoughts might turn to a long list of unwelcome outcomes: memories of what you have done in the past; thoughts of what may happen in the future.

As we all know, to play your best golf, your attention needs to be in the here and now. The present moment.

This is where the power of questions comes to the fore. Ask poor questions and you will come up with poor answers: 'How can I put a good score together if I hook my opening tee shot out of bounds?' and 'why do I always block it in the trees up the right?'

When your mind and attention start to jump into the future or delve into the past, you are no longer present to the task.

If you are thinking of hooks and blocks, your brain and body will go in search of evidence to back up that you can and probably will produce these one of these shots. What the thinker thinks, the prover proves.

Conversely, ask good questions and you will come up with good answers: 'Is it possible I could hit the fairway here at this unique moment in time right now?' and 'Is it possible that this could be the best tee shot I have ever hit?' Yes!

'What does a really good shot look like?' and 'What does a really good shot feel like?' Yes!

See the shot, feel it, trust it and commit to creating it.

We make no apologies for talking about asking good questions throughout this book. Quite the opposite. We understand the power they possess. Golf is a game of attention and questions focus your attention. Good questions can prevent your mind from traveling into the future or dwelling in the past.

We are not saying that your mind will never wander – of course it will. The real trick here is to catch it before it's too late.

To catch it before you go ahead and fire your ball left or right, before you start thinking about your latest 'magic move'. Focus on the shot not the swing.

The quality of your golf will be determined by the quality of the questions you ask yourself. Whether you are standing over your opening tee shot, your approach to the 6th or a three-foot putt on the last to win a club competition or a major championship, remember to ask good questions.

Is it possible you could hit your career-best drive, hit that approach shot to within a few feet of the flag or hole that winning putt? You bet it is.

Regardless of the situation and the consequences, you will always have the choice as to how you react to any 'pressure' situation. Choose wisely and it is entirely possible that some exceptionally good things could happen.

Pressure exists but the reality is that it only exists in your mind when you place more importance on any given situation or shot than another.

All shots are equal. While you may believe that one shot or situation has greater value than any other, if you take the approach that every shot is just another shot, this can have an incredibly powerful impact on your learning experience and your performance.

A point worth restating here is that we don't believe you can just get rid of feelings of discomfort that well up for all individuals at some point depending on their perception of the situation.

Even the very best players feel very uncomfortable at times.

The idea top players just glide round the golf course in a zen-like state of calm all of the time is utter nonsense.

What we do believe is that you can still perform with discomfort if your attention is in the right place for you as an individual.

Rather than trying to get rid of discomfort, if we embrace the feelings as 'energy' and resolve to stay with our commitment then you will find that you can perform really well in the presence of discomfort. Maybe the strongest story you can create for yourself around this is: 'I can still perform well with the feelings of discomfort'.

The Perception Of Difficulty

If we internally perceive a situation or a task to be extremely difficult then, for many of us, a degree of tightening can take place.

The standard mantra in psychology books over the years has always been to aim at the smallest possible target, the idea that if you aim at the bullseye then you will at least hit the board.

It sounds a great theory but unfortunately for many golfers it just doesn't work. If this theory works for you then by all means keep doing it but we have worked with many tour players who have challenged this notion.

An example would be that most people would be reasonably relaxed driving on a motorway but when you narrow the target to a small contraflow lane you often see drivers holding on to the steering wheel with an extra dose of tension.

Aim to experiment with this in your own game. Test it out.

Do you perform better aiming at small targets or do you free things up if you see more of a wider channel? You can try this when you practise on the range with alignment rods. Instead of putting them down at your feet have them out in front of you to create your 'channel'. See what width of channel works best for you. You can then take this mental image out onto the golf course.

For many players it is very liberating to think that all they have to do is send the ball down a relatively wide channel as opposed to aiming at a leaf on a tree.

How To Use Statistics Wisely

The vast majority of modern tournament professionals look to statistics, not only to see where they are with their own game but also to figure out how best to plot their way round any given course.

Statistics can be very helpful and there an awful lot of very smart people in the golfing world who are collecting data and creating some really useful stats.

However, there are a number of factors that can directly influence data and stats.

What we don't know is how a particular individual was feeling or thinking about standing over any given shot. What was their intention for that shot? Where was their attention? What was the situation? Were they trying to get up and down to make the cut or hole a six-foot putt to win a major? Until we know the context of the shots and data recorded, we will only really know what happened, not why it happened.

We are not knocking anyone who provides statistics, far from it.

As we said, they can be very helpful on a number of levels but until we know what was going on in a player's mind at that unique moment in time when he or she played any shot, we can only really view them as outcome statistics, not situation statistics. Context is everything.

The great Mark Twain once said: "Most people use statistics like a drunk man uses a lamppost; more for support than illumination."

We suggest you keep a record of your own fairways and greens hit in regulation in your notebook.

If you missed a fairway or green to the left or to the right, write it down. Keep a record of how many times you got up and down from the edge of the green and from greenside bunkers. Note down how many putts you had. These will all help to let you know where you are with the outcomes of a variety of shots. The data you gather will show you patterns in your play and general trends in your performance. This, however, will not tell the full story.

The next step is where you can really make a massive difference but please understand you will have to be brutally honest with yourself here in order for your stats to mean anything.

Alongside your stats, write down how you were feeling when you played certain shots.

What was the context and did that situation or context influence your choice of shot? Did you see the shot clearly? Did you fully commit to the shot or did you change your mind halfway down your downswing?

Was the drive you hit the 16th fairway with your first solid hit for weeks? Was the up-and-down from the front of the 18th green to win a tournament, the monthly medal or get your handicap cut? Without considering the situation, all you are really doing is gathering outcome patterns, which may or may not be helpful.

If you can put every shot you record into context, you can really start to make some genuine progress.

By asking good questions, such as 'what was my intention for that shot', 'did I manage to keep my attention on the task at hand' or 'was I distracted by the potential outcome' and 'what did it mean, relative to my score' you will start to see some real and relevant patterns – not only of what happened but why it happened.

Once you gain a true understanding of why as well as what, you can really start to develop and improve some incredibly powerful skills, such as attention, which will then ultimately transfer over playing to playing better golf shots when it matters.

We know that may have sidetracked you a little from our thoughts on strategy but we believe it is extremely important for you to understand that using stats and data to form a strategy or plan of attack for the golf course, has to include context.

Every Shot Matters

A very simple strategy we would encourage you to adopt is one where every single shot matters. Pay attention to each and every shot, one shot at a time.

To put things into perspective, the top 15 players on the Challenge Tour's order of merit earn a European Tour card for the following season. In 2018, the player finishing 16th missed out by €604. Over the course of a 20-odd tournament season, that is a pretty small margin that may well have been down to a couple of missed putts.

It might have been a couple of lapses in concentration at key moments. Once again, the stats will show you he came up just short but they will not tell you why.

Conversely, the guy who won the PGA Tour LatinoAmerica money list, and with it an exemption on to the Korn Ferry Tour, finished a mere $64 ahead of the guy who finished second.

Had he missed one more putt or hit a drive out of bounds at any point during the course of the season, he would not have gone down in the record books as the winner of the order of merit. Congratulations to Harry Higgs for paying sufficient attention.

Play To Learn

Play to learn rather than learn to play. The best way to figure out how you are going to find your best strategy to shoot your best possible scores is by playing the golf course.

If you hit driver off the 1st tee at your home course every time you play, see what happens when you hit 3-wood instead. If going for all the long par 4 holes in two isn't working out for you, play them as three-shot holes.

You might be pleasantly surprised at how many times you get up and down for par. If trying to hit 3-wood into par 5s when you know it is out of reach is yielding more bogeys and doubles than pars and birdies, lay up to your favourite wedge distance.

You'll soon figure it out – you're a smart person. You must be, you're reading this book after all. But seriously, rather than allowing your mind and golf game to operate in auto-pilot mode, take a moment to think about how you can play any given shot on any given hole in the most stress-free way possible.

You don't have to hit your longest drive, or hit your hybrid to 10 feet, in order to make a good score on a hole.

For most amateur golfers, the shot most likely to have the greatest influence on your scoring is the third shot. Think about where you play the majority of your third shots from and how much success you have from there.

Would your scores improve if you played better third shots? Absolutely. With that in mind, don't neglect your short game.

Being the proud owner of a red-hot short game does wonders for your confidence.

The better you are on and around the greens, the less pressure you will put the rest of your game under.

The same principles apply with the short game as they do with any other shot. Ask good questions to provide good answers. At the risk of reiterating what we covered in Chapter 4, asking the same questions of 'is it possible to play a great shot here', 'what is the shot' and 'what does that good shot look and feel like' will allow you to see, feel and create the shot required at that specific moment in time.

The better you get at creating these shots, creating a short-game library if you like, the more fun you will have both in training and on the course.

Do you think Tiger Woods won his 15th major, or any of his previous 14 major victories, without a game plan or strategy?

No chance. Do you think he figured out the best way to play every shot on every hole in every round before he set foot on the 1st tee? You bet he did.

Key Takeaways

1 A bad attitude is like a flat tyre: You can't go anywhere until you change it.

2 Preparation starts with having a plan of action and a clear intention. Only then do you have somewhere to place your attention.

3 On a range you are hitting balls into a wide-open space. As Butch Harmon said: "If you aim at nothing, you'll hit it every time."

4 Separate your round into six sets of three holes to free you from what has gone before and what lies ahead.

5 Rather than thinking of 1st tee nerves, rephrase this experience as 1st tee energy and adrenaline.

6 Experiment in your own game to find out if you perform better when aiming at small targets or if you see more of a wider channel? We're all different.

7 Statistics can be very helpful on a number of levels but context is everything.

8 For amateur golfers, the shot most likely to have the greatest influence on your scoring is the third shot. How much would your scores improve if you played better third shots?

Expert Insight

HOW THE GAME WAS PLAYED IN THE BEGINNING

A Hebridean links reminds us how the game was once, and perhaps still should be, played. By Duncan Lennard

B ACK in 2005, a precious golfing time capsule was discovered under the wind-strafed machair of South Uist in Scotland's Outer Hebrides.

The original golf course at Askernish had been designed by none other than Old Tom Morris in 1891, but fell into disuse during the 1920s after the surrounding land was adopted into crofting tenure. Though golf was played on and off in this area during the 20th century, Old Tom's original layout remained lost... and unmolested.

As such the links – painstakingly recreated by architect Martin Ebert and its discoverer, golf course consultant Gordon Irvine – offers a unique opportunity to see what golf looked like at the end of the 19th century, and to get a little closer to understanding the game Old Tom knew and played.

Of course there are plenty of other courses in the UK around this vintage and older, many designed by Old Tom; but none is in its original form.

Equipment breakthroughs, greenkeeping technologies and practices, architecture fashions, even a century of 'captain's bunkers';

all have taken their toll.

Today, every venerable old course you care to mention is the evolution of a steady stream of tweaks, updates and redesigns. Royal County Down and Muirfield are two such Old Tom courses that today have only whispers of his original design.

So, how did Old Tom's golf differ from today's?

For the modern-day visitor to Askernish, the biggest difference will likely be the sheer rawness of the course.

Cattle and sheep can graze the links in the winter, and no artificial fertilisers or herbicides are used.

In terms of its conditioning, the course is hardly any different to how it would have been presented in Old Tom's day.

Following on from the rawness is the sheer muscularity of the course. So far from avoiding severe slopes and gradients, Old Tom seemingly made a beeline for them.

He followed the same principle at dramatic Machrihanish and at Prestwick, where his art is potently illustrated by the employment of the massive Alps dune in hiding his 2nd green, the current 17th.

Played across such dramatic landscapes, these courses suffused the playing experience with the need for imagination, strategy, creativity and the reading of the land.

Allied to the sensational views these vantage points readily offered, these layouts confirmed a round of golf as an exhilarating and outward-looking experience.

And this practice didn't end at the greens.

At Askernish the 2nd green has a severe spine running across it, splitting the front from the back; the 4th green is raised, and falls away dramatically at the back; the 9th green is perched on a ridge that runs diagonally across the line of play and away from the golfer; sinfully humped, 10 and 16 have more movement than you will ever have seen on a green.

As a consequence, during a round at Askernish you can fully expect your unfair share of bad lies, crazy stances, wicked kicks, chip shots that don't seem to allow a route to the hole-side and semi-circular putts. In other words, the playing experience embodies a complete lack of interest in anything approaching fairness. Instead, it embraces the element of chance.

Yes, this was the game Old Tom Morris knew and loved. After all, he grew up using a makeshift, homemade golf club, striking wine corks nailed for weight at the lampposts that lit the roads of St Andrews. Called Sillybodkins, this was the ultimate game of resourcefulness and imagination. After all, you look pretty daft complaining of a bad lie when your fairway is North Street.

Old Tom understood that in golf control was a myth, and the pursuing of it a fool's errand. He enjoyed the chaotic nature of the game, the slings and arrows it threw up, and set his courses up to capitalise on them. This was golf distilled, a simple game of a club, a ball, a hole and the land that got in the way.

You might not score what you thought you deserved, but you'd have a whole lot of fun along the way.

In this respect, Old Tom was a trailblazer. The revered Augusta National co-creator Dr Alister MacKenzie, whose design career took off just as Old Tom was coming to the end of his life, was greatly influenced by the Old Master.

MacKenzie considered him a true golfer and sportsman, understanding and agreeing with his philosophies on golf course design and the true nature of the game. No professional since his time has ever grasped the real sporting spirit of golf architecture like he did, he wrote.

MacKenzie shared Old Tom's passion for the Old Course. He believed it offered a true test of a golfer's imagination, strategy, creativity and skill, so making it hugely enjoyable to play irrespective of ability. MacKenzie loved the complexity of the inscrutable chip, the triple-break putt and the 40-yard run off a green – it's no coincidence these shots show up at Augusta time and again.

Neither is it coincidence that both St Andrews and Augusta have regularly been accused of being unfair.

"I hate its arrogant lumps and bumps and the times you must play shots with one leg up in the air," said Neil Coles of St Andrews. "I don't like it, to tell you the truth, said Sergio Garcia of Augusta (admittedly before his 2017 victory). "I don't think it's fair, and it's just too tricky. It's too much of a guessing game."

But then MacKenzie, like Old Tom, had little interest in 'fairness'. Indeed, in The Spirit of St Andrews he wrote of rejoicing when his layouts were routinely described as unfair.

"At first I was much disturbed because no one had described Cypress Point as unfair," he wrote of his 1928 creation.

"On further consideration I came to the conclusion that the amazing beauty of Cypress Point disarmed criticism."

Now, to the habituated strokeplayer – and today, that's most of us – this type of golf is all a bit disconcerting. After all cuppy lies, bad bounces and trusting to luck are no friends of the scorecard. But when you consider the head-to-head nature of golf in Old Tom's day, Askernish and this type of golf makes more sense.

"What we can see here, and in much of Old Tom's work, is golf designed for matchplay," says Irvine. "Today, the game is played by a fraternity worrying about its handicap; if a club feels a hole is 'unfair', they will change it. But at Askernish, the landscape is so raw and muscular that rub-of-the-green forms a big part of the playing experience.

"In some respects, Askernish echoes all those lovely, quirky putting greens you'll find in every Scottish seaside town. They were set out on a piece of ground that was fun, and people putted for fun. Old Tom's golf was the same game of ball and turf, and bringing out the excitement and chance when the two interacted.

"Try to keep a score at Askernish and you'll resent its extreme contours. But go head-to-head against someone and you might just find yourself relishing the opportunity to hole the putt that sees you win a hole with an 7."

Nor was MacKenzie a lover of strokeplay. "There are many of us who firmly believe that a contest between flesh and blood is the only true form of golf, and that too much score play is detrimental to the real interest of the game," he asserted. "Surely there is far more fun in a contest against flesh and blood than against a card and pencil?"

Of course there is a great deal of satisfaction in posting a low score, and getting your handicap down. But it's a type of golf that comes with its baggage.

Scorecard golf mandates a demand for a fair playing arena, one that leads to expensively and chemically maintained fairways and greens and the removal of quirky, interesting course features. It sets golfers on a quest for control that can be so frustrating and tiresome that even people as accomplished as Bobby Jones end up describing players as "the dogged victims of inexorable fate". Sending us into elaborate and painstaking rituals of yardage calculation, of assessing lines and conditions, neither is it any friend of prompt play.

Askernish serves as a timely reminder that there is another way of playing golf – a way that removes the pressure, makes execution less laboured and more instinctive, provides a beatable opponent and, above all, increases the fun.

This was Old Tom's game, and Alister MacKenzie's. Set against the modern landscape of Planet Golf, it may seem a little outdated; yet there is surely no harm in making sure that, from time to time, it is your game too.

About The Author

Duncan Lennard is author of the best-selling Extreme Golf: The world's most unusual, fantastic and bizarre courses and its follow-up 112 Miles to the Pin. Based in Exeter, Devon, he is a regular contributor to a range of national golf publications including Golf World and Today's Golfer.

Chapter 6
CAN YOU ADJUST AND ADAPT ON THE COURSE?

Golf is an inherently unpredictable game – how do you cope with variables from an uneven stance to a bad bounce?

Adjust / əˈdʒʌst / Verb. To alter or move something slightly in order to achieve the desired result.

Adapt / əˈdapt / Verb. To adjust oneself to different conditions and/or situations.

IMAGINE this for a scenario. The temperature is warm every day. The wind never blows. The only thing visible in the blue sky above is bright, golden sunshine. Every blade of emerald-green grass on every golf course is perfectly manicured. Every lie you find in the fairway is perfectly flat. Every time your ball finishes in a bunker, it sits up perfectly. Every lie you find in the rough is exactly the same, perfect. You always have a perfect yardage from the middle of every fairway to a hole cut in the middle of the green. Every green is the same pace and all your putts are flat and straight. Positively utopian.

Sounds pretty awesome but at the same time ridiculous, right?

Of course it does, that would never happen, but please stay with us for a moment.

If this were the case, it would make total sense for you to go to work on your golf swing, hitting 20 balls on the range with each club in a bid to perfect your backswing and numerous other positions to allow you to hit the ball dead straight, exactly the same distance and direction time after time.

You could then head to the short game area to practise the same pitch shot from the same distance and the same perfect lie with the same club for half and hour before repeating the same process for chip shots.

Once you have mastered them, you could place a few balls in perfect lies in the practice bunker and repeat, repeat, repeat.

Bunker play perfected, now it would be time to head to the putting green to work on your perfectly flat, perfectly straight putts from your favourite distance of two feet.

If you believe this is the way forward, the way to become more consistent, please think again.

In all probability, you are practising shots that you will rarely face on the golf course. You may feel you have put in some time and effort and to the casual observer, you probably look like you are working really hard and deserve to reap some rewards for your efforts.

The fact of the matter is, in reality, your practice session bears virtually no resemblance to what you will encounter on any given day on any given golf course.

Yes the temperature may be to your liking certain beautiful days but everything else – including wind, uneven lies, sloping greens, breaking putts and awkward distances – will almost always be a factor. So what do you do then? Do you react or respond? How do you deal with them? Do you in fact deal with them or do you bemoan your bad luck and ill-fortune that the ball is sitting down in the rough?

You can't believe how unfair it is that you can only get one foot in the bunker and your first putt of the day looks faster than Usain Bolt! Do you complain or do you adjust and or adapt?

Take a minute or two to think about this. Are you practising for utopia or are you training for the reality and inevitability of the diverse conditions you will face and the shots you will have to create when you play golf?

Golf is the ultimate game of adjustment and adaptability. The golf course and Mother Nature demand that we have to adjust and adapt constantly, yet the majority of golfers fail to prepare or train for this inevitability.

In order to improve, you must be prepared to adjust and adapt.

Think about the last three rounds of golf you played and the shots you had to create. What percentage of those shots have you previously practised? How many of those shots required a skill you have neither trained or even thought about working on? Probably quite a few.

Would you approach any other game, pursuit or business situation in the same manner? Unlikely.

So why is it that we practice one thing then act all surprised when we have to adjust and adapt on the golf course?

The ability to adjust and adapt are skills that can be learned as you will see from Ed Coughlan in Chapter 7 but in the meantime let's stick with the concept for now.

Michael Hebron, the influential American golf coach, pointed us towards research conducted at Harvard University which reveals some very interesting insights:.

"The reason you can't move the same way each and every time, such a swinging a golf club, is that your brain can't plan the swing the same way each time," says assistant professor Krishna Shenoy, whose research includes study of the neural basis of sensorimotor integration and movement control. He co-authored this study alongside postdoctoral researcher Mark Churchland and electrical engineering doctoral candidate and medical student Afsheen Afshar.

According to Churchland: "It's as if each time the brain tries to solve the problem of how to move, it does it anew.

"Practice and training can help the brain solve the problem more capably but people and other primates simply aren't wired for consistency like computers or machines."

Why Flexibility And Adaptability Beat Consistency

For athletes in general, and golfers in particular, the inability to replicate the perfect movement might seem to be a frustrating problem that needs to be solved.

But the researchers speculate that the brain has evolved its apparently improvisational style precisely because the vast majority of situations requiring significant movements are novel.

Churchland says: "The nervous system was not designed to do the same thing over and over again. It was designed to be flexible. You typically find yourself doing things you've never done before."

Most golfers, when performing poorly, attribute their results to technique and blame their golf swing. Then they spend more time practising. Yet the survey showed that golfers who are performing well actually spend less time practising or training.

We are led to believe that we can groove or perfect our stroke or swing to the point it almost repeats on its own. However, all the research and science is telling us the brain simply will not allow this to happen.

If you can accept that your swing will always contain an element of variability, then you can pay more attention to how it functions rather than how it looks. Golf really is the most random game, one that is played in a flexible and ever-changing environment, so why practise hitting the same shot with the same swing in a fixed environment on the driving range?

Training really should be just that. Training for the inevitability of the need to adapt and be flexible and ready to make constant adjustments on the course when actually playing golf.

Does it really make any sense to work on grooving your swing or putting stroke when you know you are going to have to make slight adjustments to adapt to unique shots at unique moments in time?

Don't get us wrong, if working on your technique is paying dividends and you are winning majors, the club championship or the Sunday match with your buddies every week and shooting your best-ever scores along the way, then please continue to do exactly what you are doing.

However, if your current way of playing golf, conceptually, physically and mentally, isn't working for you, let's look at it through a different lens.

As a certain Albert Einstein famously said: "Insanity: doing the same thing over and over again and expecting different results."

Let's focus your attention on learning or acquiring skills. The term 'skill acquisition' has become increasingly more prevalent of late and we are strong believers in working towards increasing and improving golfers' skill sets rather than their golf swings.

The paradox here is that as skill sets improve, so does technique. Unfortunately, golf has historically been taught and coached the other way round. We are led to believe that as our swing improves, so will our shot-making skills.

If you are working on repeating a movement aimed at creating a consistent shot, you will be limited to that shot, or unintentional slight variations of that one shot. Not much help when you have to hit a low draw to bend your ball around and under the branches of a tree. There has to be an element of flexibility or adjustment when learning any new skill, in order for you to apply the most relevant version of that skill in that unique moment in time, appropriate to the situation and conditions.

We want to talk about creating shots, rather than 'getting it in the slot at the top of the backswing'.

Our aim is to help you understand the need to develop relevant and appropriate skills you can then apply to your game.

We are not going to prescribe the same technical skills to anyone and everyone. One size does not fit all. It never has and never will.

Just look at the swings of the top-10 ranked golfers on the planet at any given time and you will soon see that their styles are very, very different.

However, their skill sets are very, very similar. They all have their way or ways of getting the job done when they have to.

Did they find their way of creating the right shot at the right time by accident? Highly unlikely. They developed these skills through practice and training both on the range and on the course.

More often than not, these learning experiences actually happen during tournament play. We learn from our mistakes. Regardless of what they are or where they happen, mistakes can be used to either fuel your frustration or direct your attention to exploring how you could solve a particular puzzle or problem. We would obviously recommend the latter approach.

With each and every training session you embark on, you should have a very clear intention that includes an element of exploration and experimentation. We are not suggesting you try to do something totally different on each and every shot but you may want to make a slight adjustment or adaptation to the previous shot if it didn't quite match up to your original intention, whatever that may have been.

If your intention was a fade, for example, and the resultant shot was a straight pull which started left (for a right-hander) and stayed there, rather than changing your swing and trying something entirely different, think about it for a moment or two.

Chances are, the shot you just pulled was the result of the path and face both pointing left at impact.

Now, if you were to place your focused attention on slightly adjusting the face so it is slightly open to the path at impact on the next shot then, should you manage to find the middle of the clubface, the resultant shot will start slightly left then curve back towards your intended target. Do this successfully and will have enjoyed the experience of adjusting and adapting in its simplest form. What a great learning experience that is.

Not only is it educational, it is also extremely rewarding and enjoyable. In various sports, in business and indeed in any discipline, the best performers tend to be the best learners. They also tend to be the best at adjusting and adapting to whatever the task in front of them happens to be.

View your practice and training sessions as opportunities to explore different ways of creating the same or similar end results or outcomes. That is what consistency really means, not repeating the same movement time after time, ball after ball, shot after shot.

Not only will the time you spend experimenting be a whole lot of fun, when you have a very clear intention of the shots you want to create during these sessions and can bring the shots to life, you will be rewarded with an incredible sense of achievement.

Jack Nicklaus says in his book My Story: "I haven't fundamentally changed my swing since I was 13 years old but I've never stopped trying to increase my versatility as a shot-maker. Golf is a game of constant adjustment. The guys who adjust to the conditions and situations the best tend to be the most successful."

Creating consistent results is what all top performers do but they rarely do it through repetition.

They achieve it through finding the right way for them, at the right time. They may not feel their best or be in possession of their A-game but they know how to get over the line.

There will be days when you just don't feel it, so therefore you need to make a slight adjustment. You need to adapt what you have on any given day on any given shot.

You only need to look to the animal kingdom to see this concept in its purest form. Do you think a lion kills its prey in exactly the same manner every time? Doubtful. It will adapt and adjust depending on the situation and on the prey it is hunting.

Would it take down a zebra in the same way it would a giraffe or a buffalo? Of course not. The intention would be the same but the execution of that intention would differ according to the circumstances and the environment. The lion would figure out the best and most efficient way to achieve its goal – dinner.

A concept we love and encourage the golfers we work with to explore is one of creating a library of golf shots that you can draw upon at the appropriate moment in time. Sometimes the shot you face will require a slightly lower flight, when playing into the wind, for example, or when you are trying to land your approach shot short of the green and run it up towards the flag.

There will be occasions on the course when the shot requires you to start the ball down the left-hand side of the fairway from the tee to allow a left-to-right crosswind to drift your ball back towards your intended target in the fairway. Unless you learn how to create and play these shots in practice, unless you train these shots, you may well struggle when the moment comes on the course.

Anyone who has played any amount of links golf will know exactly where we are coming from with this.

Once you have physically created a library of shots – high fades, low draws, chip and runs, lob shots and so on – with various different clubs, remember what these shots look and feel like.

In fact, we strongly recommend you make notes.

Take time to write down what your intention was, what that shot looked like, what it felt like, and whether it matched up to your expectation and visualisation.

We suggest you write your findings down in a notebook rather than on your phone. They could easily get lost among a thousand other things in your phone but if you have a specific training notebook, you will know exactly where to find them.

Note down how you were feeling that day. Write down what the wind direction and strength was. Over a period of time you will start to see patterns form of how well you are able to create certain shots. You can mark them out of 10 for example.

Not only will this act as a fantastic reminder of how you feel or felt when you played a certain shape or height of shot, it will provide evidence of how competent you are on specific shots.

Competence leads to confidence and we all know how important a role confidence plays on the golf course.

Your journal will also serve as an excellent reference book. Your very own reference book. Use this wisely and you can start to develop your own training games.

Practice can be boring but creating and playing training games are extremely rewarding and a whole lot of fun. Aren't these two of the reasons you decided to play golf in the first place?

If you can design, or co-design, some training games with help or input from a good golf coach, you will then take ownership of and responsibility for them. Taking ownership will provide you with a sense of pride and you might just start to look at yourself in a different, more positive light. You can become an innovator. In addition to creating different shots as part of your training programme, think about creating different scenarios in your mind.

Is this shot your approach shot into the last green when you need to make par to win a tournament, or the Sunday morning match with your buddies? What is the context of the shot? Could it be that this shot could be the one that helps to get your handicap cut to single figures for the first time in your life? Is it possible that this could be the best shot you have ever hit?

Whatever the shot, scenario or situation is, write down a few questions relevant to that shot:

- What is the shot here?
- What does the ball need to do to reach its intended target?
- What does that shot look and feel like?
- What club is required to create this shot?
- How am I going to react or respond to the outcome of this shot?

These questions help to form a very clear intention, which, in turn, allows you to place your focused attention on the task you are about to perform and the shot you are about to create.

Questions focus your attention. When you are answering these questions, you will not be thinking of anything else. You will become engaged and absorbed in the task of creating a unique shot in a unique moment of time without distraction.

Do You Treat Yourself With Respect?

We make no apologies for repeatedly reinforcing the importance of having a crystal-clear intention and a single point of focussed attention. Distraction is the polar opposite and enemy of attention. It would be easy to say that you should avoid distractions at all costs but that is easier said than done.

Think about your favourite piece of music. Can you hear it in your head? That is a prime example of distraction.

By asking that question, we distracted you from this book. It is very easy to become distracted on the golf course and indeed in any situation. However, we can bring your attention back to the task in hand, which is to read this page, by asking you a few questions about your self-talk when it comes to golf.

- When you hit a good shot do your praise yourself?
- When you hit a shot that doesn't quite go to plan, do you berate yourself?
- Do you get angry?
- Do you call yourself an idiot?

You should also think about how you talk to yourself on the range when hitting shots. If your self-talk on the range isn't great, the chances are that all you are really doing is training for how you are going to talk to yourself on the course, before, during, after and between shots.

How many times has one of your playing partners complimented you on one of your tee shots that finds the middle of the fairway, only for you to respond: "Yes but I didn't quite catch it out the middle."

How would you react to a compliment from one of your playing partners if they said: "Great shot, Charlie," only to follow it up with: 'But you didn't quite catch it did you?"

It is highly unlikely you would react in an enthusiastic and positive manner. You would be more likely to think: 'What a cheek, how dare they!'

Can you see where we are going here? We sometimes talk to ourselves in a way we wouldn't dream of talking to anyone else.

The way we talk to ourselves can massively influence both our attitude and ability to develop and perform.

If you keep telling yourself that you are an incompetent, useless idiot, you will start to behave and play like one – thinker and prover.

The way you react to your shots can and will influence future shots.

If, for example, you miss a green three yards short and five yards right with a 7-iron, you might class that as a bad shot, which is an opinion. Science will tell you that opinions tend to lead to emotions. Considering a slight miss or misjudgement to be bad rarely leads to positive emotions, reactions or responses.

To go from bad to good, which are at opposite ends of the

spectrum, you must climb a mountain, cross a desert and swim an ocean. That is quite a journey.

That fact of the matter is that you have missed the green three yards short and five yards right.

We would far rather you deal in facts. If your response to that fact is 'Ok, I only slightly misjudged that', your journey is now only three yards long and five yards wide. This sounds like a much shorter and more achievable journey than having to travel from bad to good.

If you were only slightly out this time, you can rest assured that you only need to make a slight adjustment the next time you are faced with a similar shot rather than having to deconstruct and reconstruct your entire golf swing.

The way you deal with each and every shot can do one of two things. It can contaminate the next one, which is never good; or it can allow you to move on if you accept it and direct and apply your attention to the next one. The choice is yours. We strongly suggest you opt for acceptance.

As human beings, one of our first instincts is to pass judgement, good or bad. That will happen when you hit golf shots but the trick here is to be aware of that, to catch yourself. Assess rather than judge.

If you are still judging and berating yourself for the 'bad' shot that missed the green, the reality is that you are not giving yourself much of a chance with your chip or pitch shot as your attention is still on the previous shot.

If, however, you can accept you were slightly out with your approach shot, you will have already moved on and started asking questions regarding what the ball has to do on your next shot.

By simply asking the questions outlined previously, your attention will now be on the task facing you, enabling you to become totally absorbed in what that next shot looks and feels like.

You can now engage in the art of creating your chip or pitch shot.

The late, great Ben Hogan famously said: "The most important shot is the next one."

We all kind of knew what he was saying but when you put it into this context, you can really see where he was coming from with that statement. Mr Hogan was a very wise man.

How Is Your Attitude On The Golf Course?

Much has been written and said about how attitude can influence performance, not only in golf but life in general.

More often than not, we are advised to adopt a PMA – a Positive Mental Attitude. In theory, that sounds great. Better to be positive than negative right? Yes – to a degree. At some point in our lives most of us have decided to take this approach and 'think positively'.

The problem is that you can go out with an incredibly positive attitude but for any number of reasons, it might not work out for you. You can decide that on any given day you are going to hit every fairway, every green and hole every single putt you look at.

When that doesn't happen, maintaining that positive attitude is somewhat challenging.

When it lets you down, in all likelihood, you will go straight from having a positive attitude to a negative one. There is no grey area here, no middle ground.

Having coached thousands of golfers since the 1980s, including dozens of tour pros, Ryder Cup players and winners of major championships, it would not be unfair to say we have seen our fair share of bad attitudes.

What creates and or forms a bad attitude? Generally speaking, a bad attitude rears its ugly head when we form a negative opinion based on an observation. For example, we may have our golf ball derailed from going in the hole on the 1st green because it hit an unprepared pitchmark.

Rather than accept this happened due to another person's inability to fix their pitchmark, we blame the greens, the greenkeeper and even the greenkeeper's parents for having them in the first place.

We then start to look for other imperfections or blemishes in other areas of the course. We start to see that the tee markers aren't exactly perpendicular to the middle of the fairway. We notice that one of the guys in the group ahead didn't rake the greenside bunker on the 3rd hole properly. Worse than that, the guys in the group ahead of them are holding up the whole course.

Totally unacceptable – and now you're getting frustrated and angry. Before you know it, all you can see are negatives. Nothing is right. The wind only gusts when it's your turn to play. Your ball took a shocking bounce and finished just out of bounds, despite the fact that the OB posts are 50 yards right of where you were aiming. Why me? Why do these things always happen to me?

One bad shot, hole or round leads to another because you have allowed one shot, hole or round to contaminate the next one.

This bad attitude can very quickly develop into anger, which, in turn, creates negativity.

When was the last time you did something constructive when you were feeling angry or negative? Exactly – never.

It all boils down to two of the main themes of this book: Intention and Attention. If your intention is to find fault with everything and everyone, your attention will be drawn and directed to doing just that. It is all too easy to fall into the trap of seeing the downside of everything and reacting to that in a negative manner.

If positive thinking is not the way forward then what is? Rather than thinking positively, we talk elsewhere in the book about asking positive questions. When you ask positive questions, you tend to come up with good answers. What is the shot required here? Is it possible you could hit a great shot here? What does a really good shot look and feel like? We make no apologies for repeating the importance of asking good or positive questions.

A bad attitude may well start to develop at any given time in any given situation but you possess the power to thwart it and get yourself back on track. Get back to the here and now.

Questions focus your attention and in turn can have a direct and useful influence on your attitude and consequently, your behaviour and performance.

We always have a choice as to how we are going to behave. We have the choice of adopting a good or bad attitude. When you wake up in the morning, you can choose how you are going to tackle that day. Choose wisely.

The same principle applies on the golf course. Be aware of what can allow you to fall down the rabbit hole of bemoaning your bad luck which can and almost definitely will sooner or later develop into a bad attitude, anger and negativity.

The trick here is catch yourself before you go too far off track and start asking appropriate and pertinent questions to bring your attention back to where it is useful. Namely, the present moment. In reality, this is the only time we can actually make a difference.

We've all played with the guy with the bad attitude whose negativity is infectious and contagious. Before we know it, we have allowed that person's attitude and behaviour to negatively influence our own behaviour and performance.

If you really want to get the best out of yourself, don't be the person with the bad attitude. Apart from ruining your own enjoyment, you will in all likelihood spoil your playing partners' day as well. Do you really want to be responsible for that?

Reaction Tools

Here are some ideas to help you take responsibility for your reactions.

Tiger's 10-Yard Line

It was said that when Tiger Woods totally dominated the game in the early 2000s he employed this technique. The deal he made with himself was that he would hit a shot and the outcome would be what it would be. However, if he needed to let off some steam then so be it but he would see in front of the shot a line ten yards ahead. His promise to himself was that by the time he walked over that 10-yard line the previous shot was done. It was a case of releasing any necessary emotion and having a mental construct of this 10-yard line to help him 'shed' the residue of the previous shot.

Mind Your Body Language

The research of Amy Cuddy has highlighted the tremendous effect our body language has on the way we feel. When the body drops its posture we are more likely to release cortisol into our system, our stress hormone.

As we elevate our posture we tend to release more testosterone. This release tends to make us feel more in control and able to deal with whatever is being thrown at us.

If you think of how most golfers react after a poor shot, they drop their head and go into an internal dialogue that is anything but positive. A simple solution to this we have found really effective is to make the commitment that no matter what the golf ball has done you are going to walk down the fairway with your eyes above the level of the flag.

This simple procedure has the effect of improving your posture while at the same time limiting our negative internal dialogue.

Facts Not Opinions

If you are going to say anything to yourself after a shot give yourself a golden rule: make it facts, not opinions.

Calling yourself an idiot or a useless clown is just your opinion. It may seem really true at the time but does it serve you in any way?

Keep to the facts in the sense of what happened to the shot. Did you hit it heavy or thin? Was it a toe or a heel strike? Was it the wrong club?

Deal in the reality of what happened within the interaction of ball and club and you will then be able to release what has just happened and move on.

Opinions of your validity to even call yourself a golfer lead nowhere other than a spiral of negativity.

Key Takeaways

1 In all probability, you are practising shots that you will rarely face on the golf course.

2 Accept that your swing will always contain an element of variability. Pay more attention to how it functions rather than how it looks.

3 Create a library of shots that you can draw upon at the appropriate moment in time. Once you have created this library of high fades, low draws, chip and runs, lob shots and so on – with various different clubs – remember what these shots look and feel like.

4 The way we talk to ourselves can massively influence both our attitude and ability to develop and perform. If you keep telling yourself that you are an incompetent, useless idiot, you will start to behave and play like one.

5 The most important shot is always the next one.

Expert Insight

INTENTION, ACCEPTANCE AND WHAT IS POSSIBLE

At the 2019 Indian Open, Stephen Gallacher ran up an eight on Sunday yet went on to win. We asked him how

W HEN you are watching golf on TV, it is all too easy to get drawn into the analysis of a player's swing or technique and start making assumptions and drawing conclusions as to why their golf ball is behaving in a certain manner.

If you put four golf coaches in the same room, watching the same player hit a certain shot, they will almost all see what that player is doing through the lens of what they perceive to be happening.

They will all have their own ideas of what is right and wrong and they may all be correct but without knowing what that player's intention is, all anyone can really do is guess.

It may be an educated guess based on a level of knowledge and experience but it is still, in reality a guess. To understand really and truly why that player's shots do what they do, first of all you need to understand what is going on in their mind.

What is their intention and where are they placing their attention?

Two days after the conclusion of the 2019 Hero Indian Open, we spoke to the winner of that tournament, Stephen Gallacher.

What was remarkable about the Scotsman's victory was that he had a quadruple-bogey eight on the 7th hole of his final round.

It might be the only time a player on the European Tour has made an eight in the final round and gone on to win the tournament.

When we asked him about his play that week, he said: "All you can really do at this level is get into contention as often as you can and hope that your time will come.

"In order to do that, you need to hit an awful lot of good shots and hole your share of putts. A 72-hole tournament is basically an accumulation of good shots, one shot at a time."

Having struggled for form in the early part of the season, Gallacher explained that he had been fighting what he refers to as "the big miss, or the double cross".

This happens either when you aim left to hit a fade and hit a pull draw that starts left and goes further left, or when you aim right to draw the shot and the ball starts right and goes further right. Neither shot is pretty or good for your confidence.

Stephen is a smart, diligent guy and spent time with his coach to understand why this was happening. Just as you will read elsewhere in this book, his issue was not his golf swing, he had simply lost control of the clubface through impact.

Armed with that knowledge, he set about controlling it. Once his attention had been drawn to the fact that it was nothing more complex or sinister than the clubface, he then started to pay particular attention to that in his training and practice.

In a very frank and honest conversation, Stephen said: "You have to be aware of and understand your shot tendencies and accept that every now and then you will hit a bad shot. We're human beings after all.

"At our level, the bad shots might not be all that destructive but they are maybe not quite what you visualised or intended. The key here is to accept that. Over the years, I have learned that acceptance is massive. It is essential. If you can accept what happens – good, bad or indifferent – you can move on to the next shot.

"If you are still thinking about the last shot, you can't possibly focus on or pay attention to the next one. If you are still angry with yourself because you just hit a bad shot, that one bad shot can turn into a run of bad shots, bad holes and bogeys."

After taking eight on the par-4 7th, Stephen turned to his son, Jack, who was caddying for him and said: "We're only five shots back here and anything can happen on this course in these tough, windy conditions. We can still win this. Let's see if we can post a score and see what happens."

What happened was that, after accepting his eight, he did not accept his potential fate. He did not let this spoil his round, his day or his week.

He went on to play the next 11 holes in five under par, including a brave birdie on the 18th to shoot a one-under-par 71 and win by a shot. What a fantastic lesson in acceptance, resilience and what is possible with the right mindset.

When we asked him how he managed to reset and compose himself over the remaining holes, he answered: "All I did was go back to what I had been doing all week. The preparation for each shot was the same. I would get my number (yardage), talk through the shot with Jack then, once I was over the ball, my entire focus was on the target. I had no technical thoughts. I never really do when I play my best. All my focus was external, all on the target.

"This allowed me to get really tuned into creating the shot I needed to play at that particular moment in time," he said.

About Stephen Gallacher

Stephen Gallacher is a four-time European Tour winner who represented Europe in the 2014 Ryder Cup player on home soil at Gleneagles. His motto is 'enjoy life, play golf' and he does an incredible amount of great work passing on his lessons learned from playing golf at the very highest level to the kids involved in his junior foundation programme. Learn more at **sgfoundation.co.uk**

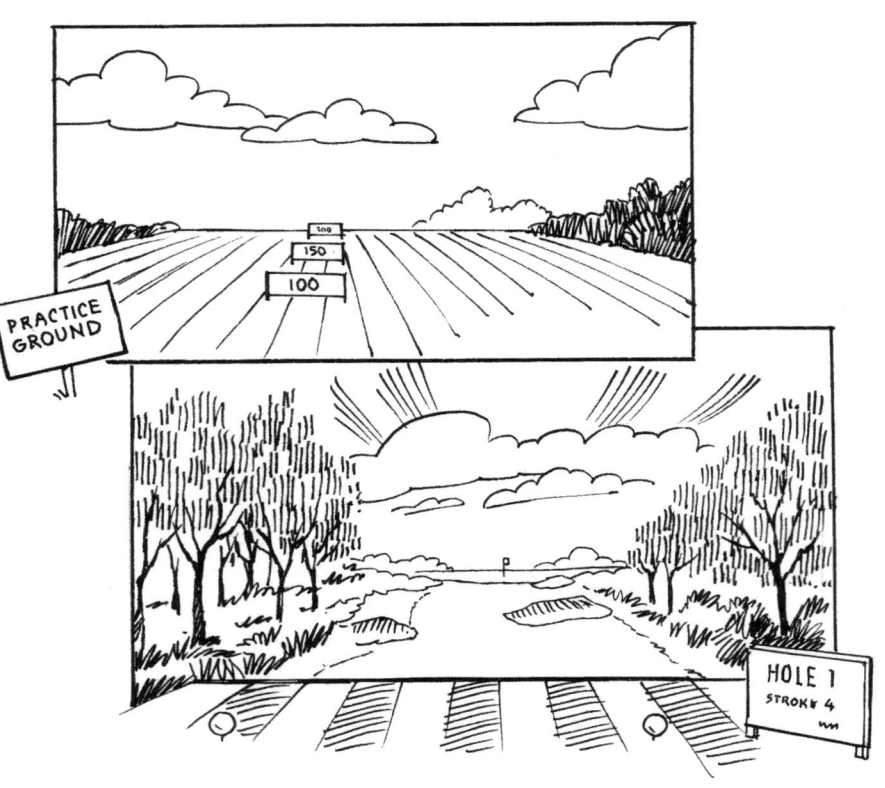

Chapter 7

IS PRACTISING GOLF THE SAME AS TRAINING FOR GOLF?

Understanding the science behind the art of preparing for golf can help you use your precious time more effectively

WE believe we would never have had the roles in golf we are fortunate to have if golfers trained better. There can be no other sport where so much effort in practice goes so unrewarded in the game itself.

Many golfers spend their entire life working hard at their game with little to no actual progress.

This cannot be because we don't have the ability to move our body in a certain way. It certainly isn't the equipment, which is so very much superior these days. For us, it is to a large degree because golfers have no real idea of how to train effectively.

We say 'train' because it is a major distinction in this book.

Instead of thinking you are going to go practising golf as you have always done, when you think in terms of training for the game you open up a whole new dimension. A surgeon will train to become a surgeon and then he or she will practise surgery. A lawyer will train to be a lawyer and then he or she will practise law.

We want you to shift your mindset completely so you train to play golf and then go and practise being a golfer on a golf course.

You become a golfer by creating golf shots in the only place that really matters – the golf course.

Go on YouTube and there will be hundreds if not thousands of experts telling you how you should move your body, what positions the club should be in, using all of the fancy terms for angles and planes, yet we promise you very little video space will be informing you of how to train in a way that will maximise your return on investment both in terms of time and money.

This book does just that. We will explain some of the science of how to train and then we will leave you to go and create the art of playing great golf.

The research is very clear: if we want to take our golf game onto the course itself we need to understand how we learn, we need to understand how to transfer skills but above all we need to learn how to train effectively. The most exciting part of this adventure is just what could be possible for you in the future. We firmly believe that no matter what your age is you could, in the next 12 months, transform your game and release the golfer in you that has been hiding away all of this time.

When you fully grasp the concept of training for golf you will get the opportunity to write a completely different story. You will become the director of your future golfing performance.

When Your Shots On The Course Don't Match Your Shots On The Range

Do you feel you have spent a good part of your golfing journey hitting the ball reasonably well on the range and yet the ability you show doesn't ever seem to transfer to the golf course when it really matters? Join the club.

So many of us have lived through the endless frustration of not being able to take our range game with us to the course.

The cycle usually goes something like this:

We have a golf lesson. We get told to do something in our swing.

We go to the range and start to work on this new move. After a while we maybe start to hit the ball better and we feel like we are getting somewhere. All we have to do is then take this particular swing thought to the course and we will be fine.

We get to the 1st tee and try to think about the same swing thought that worked so well on the range. Yet the swing doesn't seem to feel the same and the ball certainly doesn't behave in the same way.

We start dropping shots and we get frustrated. We try harder to make the swing thought work. We get worse. We go back to the range to work on our swing a little bit more. Sound familiar?

It is perhaps the universal complaint of golfers all over the world.

We can either keep doing the same thing and hope for a different result or we can step out of the loop of insanity and do something different.

The key concept to understand is that of transferability.

Does the work you do on the range, putting and chipping green actually stand a chance to transfer to the golf course?

We firmly believe that if you embrace the principles we will share with you here that you will make some real and genuine progress with your game. You will start to see some benefit from your range time as opposed to endless frustration.

The Shot Creates The Swing

Just ponder this for a moment. If the swing creates the shot, then you have to get your body to make a series of predetermined movements to produce the shot you want. However, if the shot creates the swing, could it be that if you have a clear idea of the shot you are about to play then your body will 'organise' the movements to make that happen?

Just as your body would 'organise' throwing a ball from here to there. Suddenly we then begin to ask some different questions about our game. Instead of asking 'what is wrong with my swing?' we can begin to ask 'what is wrong with my shots?' The problem with asking 'what is wrong with my swing?' is we never really get to a definitive answer. However, if we ask 'what is wrong with my shots?' then we can indeed move in a direction that has some solutions.

Of course, just by picturing a draw it doesn't mean that everyone will be able to hit one. Yet if we do picture that draw and a different shape emerges we can begin to explore what we actually need to do with the club to assist in getting the shape we desire.

There is a famous phrase attributed to the great Sam Snead.

Slammin' Sam was asked: "What do you do when you are hooking the ball?"

Snead replied: "I just go to the range and slice it for a while."

In what seems a trite comment there is real wisdom.

When a swing is producing poor shots to the left or to the right it is out of balance.

With a slice, the path is too far to the left and the face is pointing too far to the right. When you aim to hit the opposite shot a hook you do the opposite. You close the face to the path and send the path more to the right.

By aiming to do the complete opposite you bring your swing back into balance. In this way the shot can actually fix the swing.

So much golf instruction tends to be skewed towards how a swing looks. A coach will put your swing up on a screen and compare it to an expert model. That model is not you and never will be.

Your golf swing is, or should be, as unique as your fingerprint or your signature. The only thing that really matters with your golf swing is: Do you have the skill to apply the club in a certain way to produce a certain shot? All else is irrelevant.

You may say Jim Furyk doesn't have great style in his swing – but boy does he have some skill when it comes to applying the club to produce golf shots.

Your training on the range should be about developing greater skills and much less about getting into positions deemed as important by someone other than yourself.

A key concept in developing skills is the idea of 'trapping the feeling'. We get it right by feeling what is wrong. So many golfers interrupt natural learning by always trying to get it 'right'.

The brain doesn't learn that way. A baby doesn't learn to walk by getting it 'right'. A baby learns to walk by getting up from a crawl then falling to the left, falling to the right over and over again then eventually the nervous system 'traps' the feeling and organises movement and we have the miracle of being able to walk.

Begin to think of building your golf skills in a similar way.

So 'mistakes' are not only not to be afraid of they are positively essential in the quest to build effective golfing skill. When your brain can sense what is wrong, it can also sense what is right.

Notes On Training

Perhaps the single most important concept in your training is that of attention. What you put your attention on will be absolutely critical to your progress and perhaps even more importantly how you focus your attention.

The ability to have your attention in the right place to get the job done is central to becoming the best player you can be.

We want you to become an attention detective in the sense of finding out where and how you need to focus your attention to make you tick as a unique individual.

Take ownership of your attention and you will take ownership of your game.

Much research has been done on skill acquisition and the placing of your attention. Gabrielle Wulf has spent her entire academic life studying the effects of attentional focus. She has looked in particular at the effect of what she calls internal versus external focus.

Put simply, internal focus, in terms of movement skills, is when you are focussing your attention on a part of your body.

So, in golfing terms, this would be something like focussing on turning your hips or your shoulders or hinging your wrists.

Basically, you are aiming to move your body in a different way by focussing your attention there.

An external focus means concentrating on outcome or the effect of a movement.

So, in golf, this could be the ball flight or the target or it could be what you intend to do with the golf club.

Basically, external focus is a 'where' focus, whereas internal focus is a 'how' focus.

The relationship between focus and performance is clear: Numerous studies have shown that an external focus leads to a better performance than an internal focus.

From Wulf we learn that:

- An external focus stimulates an automatic type of motor control by using reflexive and subconscious processes
- An internal focus intervenes in the process that controls the coordination of a movement

The science suggests that external focus does not interfere with the self-organization process which is another way of describing spontaneous movement. Internal focus, on the other hand, does interfere with these processes. Science shows that most exceptional performance is down to an external focus.

What Goes Wrong Under Pressure?

A significant amount of research is showing that in a tournament it is not so much 'the pressure' which is important but far more about where your focus goes. It would seem that we can get the job done in the face of discomfort if we maintain more of an external focus.

What many players do when they feel the heat, be that in a monthly medal or a major tournament, is shift to an internal focus and start to think about how they are going to make a swing instead of what they actually want to create in terms of a golf shot.

Two Unconventional But Powerful Approaches To Effective Learning

1 Differential Learning

The accepted model of golf practice is that we stand on a range and try to repeat a movement over and over again in the belief that our brain will remember the good swings and code these swings into our system. Maybe you have tried this for a number of years and you have had spectacular results. If so then you need to keep going with this approach.

However, if you find, as many do, that you have an inability to transfer your skills then it could be time to develop some flexibility in your approach.

We are not saying you should completely throw all block practice out of the window but there is a very interesting approach that has yielded some incredible results when tested.

It is totally counterintuitive and goes against all existing norms and ideas but differential learning could potentially open up a very interesting window into your training schedule.

In a differential training session you only make one 'normal' swing in the session; everything after that is a variation.

You change something on every shot – your grip, alignment, ball position. Perhaps you even play a shot one-handed or cross-handed. You might change the target or the shape. Every single shot is up to you to create.

We know that it sounds weird and a bit wacky but the research suggests this approach creates a lot of noise in the nervous system. It is disruptive and our system is forced to handle lots of new information and sensations.

It is then in the face of all of this 'noise' that learning takes place and then when the system settles back down it is able to adapt much better to creating this shot in this moment.

It is totally counter to what many currently believe but is it not what kids do when they experience fantastic progress in a short space of time? Kids just go out and create lots of different shots.

They don't want to be bored hitting the same shot over and over again. The system is subjected to tremendous variety and the response is genuine learning.

We then become adults and all of that is forgotten.

We are grateful to our colleague Markus Westerburg who shared this fantastic research into the discipline of the shot put.

His book is called 'The Golfers Sixth Sense' and is an essential addition to your golfing library.

The Shot Put Study by Beckmann and Schollhorn tested a differential learning approach with the shot put.

The study wanted to compare a traditional approach to shot put training with a differential learning approach.

Twenty-four subjects were tested on their shot put distance and divided into two equal groups for eight training sessions over four weeks. One group would be trained using traditional methods and the other differential methods.

Three follow-up tests were used to determine each athlete's development: one at the end of training, one two weeks later and the last four weeks after training had been completed.

In the test at the end of Week Four, the Traditional group had increased their shot put distance by about seven inches (or 3 per cent) from 21.4 feet to 22 feet. The Differential group had increased their shot put distance by 22 inches (or 9 per cent) 21.4 feet to 23.2 feet. These results were interesting but not as interesting as the follow ups.

The groups were tested two more times even though they didn't train any more after Week Four.

In the test at the end of Week Six, the Traditional group had gone back to where they started at 21.4 feet. The Differential group had further increased their distance from the Week Four test even though they hadn't trained for two weeks. The average shot put distance was now 23.5 feet – a 10 per cent increase.

Finally, in the test at the end of Week Eight, the Traditional group stayed at the same distance of 21.4 feet. The Differential group had again increased from the last test and now had an average shot put distance of 23.7 feet without any training for four weeks.

At the end of the testing, the Differential learning group had increased their shot put distance by 28.3 inches while the Traditional group had not improved at all. Absolutely remarkable results and hard to understand. The complete opposite of what we have been led to believe in the quest for the elusive consistency.

Could it be that by creating such a wide range of experiences for the nervous system, by creating so much 'noise' within the system, that when you then return to swinging the club in a 'standard' way your ability to do just that improves.

A metaphor for us would be similar to training in a gym when you 'overload' a muscle. When you stress it in the right way the muscles adapts and grows back stronger.

2 Movement Economy

A whole body of research has shown accuracy is best achieved in sport with an external focus.

However, one study tested both accuracy and movement economy.

The researchers investigated how focus affected muscular activity and shooting accuracy with a basketball free throw.

The internal focus group was told to focus on 'the snap of their wrist' while the external group was told to focus attention on the 'centre of the rear of the basketball hoop'

The results were in line with previous findings. The external focus gave less muscle activity and better shooting precision. The most interesting finding was that not only did the internal focus group have a higher muscle activity than the external focus group in the wrist flexor of the shooting hand (Flexor Capri Radialis) but also in surrounding muscles such as arm flexor (Biceps) and extender (Triceps Brachii).

These findings suggest an internal focus of attention activates more parts of the body than just the one in focus.

Consequently a golfer who thinks about turning his shoulders might activate more muscles than just those of his shoulders, which in turn could affect the whole of his swing.

3 The Constraints-led Approach

The constraints-led approach to training is a form of implicit learning in so much that you will be making changes to your game without necessarily being consciously aware of it.

In effect, a constraint is a problem or a puzzle set up in your environment to get you to do something different than your normal pattern or habit.

For instance, in tennis if a player wanted to change a part of their service action, instead of working on all of the minute details of what arms, wrists and body are doing they would put cones in one half of the service area so the actual landing of the tennis ball was severely restricted. Thus change takes place in the action as a result of trying to solve a problem.

In golf the classic example would be a slicer. The slicer has spent most of their golfing life swinging to the left because of an open clubface. They fear the right side of the golf course so the subconscious mind makes them swing to the left. The ball starts left and then curves to the right. To swing the club out to the right feels really scary because that is where most of their bad shots end up.

However, if you stand a slicer next to a tree that is to their left they then cannot start the ball in their usual way. The tree is a constraint and so they now have a problem to solve.

It is amazing in such situations how the unconscious mind gets to work and creates new movement. You will be changing your pattern of movement as a result of an outside constraint.

Exactly the same principle would apply for someone who hooks the ball. They have a path that is too far to the right as a result of a closed clubface.

This time the tree needs to be to the right of the player and so blocking the natural pattern of starting the ball way to the right.

Movement has to be organised around the constraint.

The path becomes more neutral and straighter shots ensue.

One of the keys with the constraints-led approach is that you don't cheat by altering your alignment.

You are only limited by your imagination with the constraints-led approach. You could create a later release in the swing by again using the tree and having to hit a ball under a branch without resorting to putting the ball back in your stance.

The low branch forces you to release the club later and create a lower ball flight.

The wonderful thing about this approach is that it enhances creativity and allows you to change movement with little or no conscious interference.

In Conclusion

The whole purpose of training for golf should be to get you ready to play the real game itself.

The key aspect of training, and the only question that really matters, is: Does this transfer to the golf course?

If you consistently hit good shots on the range and you rarely take this ability with you to the course then it is not so much your skills that are the issue but more about the way you train.

Practising in the conventional way is seductive and, we would go as far as to say, addictive.

You go to a place you feel comfortable. It is usually a nice quiet environment and after a few shots you get into the rhythm of hitting good 5-irons or 7-irons. The shots feel good and so do you.

One point we would make here is that if you do this kind of practice and it brings you a great deal of pleasure and you have no real interest in lower scores or handicap reductions then you should by all means keep doing it. We don't want to rob you of your pleasure.

That said, if lower scores and improvement are your goals then hopefully these suggestions will really resonate and give you a new direction and a new way to approach the game. We are absolutely convinced that if you do take this approach then you have the chance to experience something very special in the future.

How good will it feel to have a genuine breakthrough, to take your game to another level?

How proud would you be to have actually changed your patterns and habits and produced the kind of results you deep down knew were possible?

Key Takeaways

1 Shift your mindset so you train to play golf and then go and practise being a golfer on a golf course.

2 You become a golfer by creating golf shots in the only place that really matters – the golf course.

3 We have become range experts but golf course dummies. All our 'on course' training is designed to get both your mind and your body ready for the scenarios golf throws up.

4 Internal focus is when you are focussing your attention on a part of your body. An external focus means concentrating on outcome or the effect of a movement. External focus is a 'where' focus, whereas internal focus is a 'how' focus. Numerous studies have shown that an external focus leads to better performance.

5 The whole purpose of training for golf should be to get you ready to play the real game itself.

THE LOST ART OF PRACTICE

*Are you sure your practice is representative of the challenges
you face when you play, asks Ed Coughlan*

ALLOW me to take you on a trip down memory lane, back to
when you played like a child with little or no encouragement.
If your golfing childhood was anything like mine, it was filled with
vivid pictures in your head that set the scene and went a long way
towards convincing you and your playmates that you were right in
the middle of whatever famous sporting occasion you had most
recently seen on TV.

In spring, it was Augusta for the Masters and Lansdowne Road
for the Five Nations rugby. In summer, it was Wimbledon and the
Open Championship (especially when it was back at the home of
golf in St Andrews), and nothing quite beat the intensity and the
range of games played during a football World Cup or Olympic
Games. Each generation will have its heroes that sparked such
enthusiastic recreation and creativity to set up Amen Corner in the
back garden or Centre Court on the street.

Remarkably, but not by accident, we used to set up games that
were perfectly pitched for our ability, if not a little ahead of what we
were capable of at that time.

Teams were rarely uneven, and if they turned out that way, adjustments were made with little fuss, to maintain a healthy level of competition throughout.

There was always a consequence when you lost (the pettier, the better) and we believed every shot mattered, every play was massive and every decision was a turning point.

Because we believed so fervently, tensions rose from time to time and those who did not learn quickly enough how to control their emotions had their buttons pressed in just the right way the next time to set them off again and ultimately swing the game.

The problem-solving was intricate, the decision-making limitless and the lessons learned endless.

The environment was also ever-changing as an advantage for one person was never allowed to ruin the game, so rules were constantly changing. In fact, such rule changes were quickly accepted, as it suggested this person was worthy of such constraints, a badge of honour per se.

Finally, a consistent sound heard throughout such carefree days was a running commentary of what was unfolding and an almost seamless switch of the narrative from the commentary box to the player's point-of-view.

The total immersive environment was set for all manner of brilliance to shine through, and there was not a coach in sight.

Everyone's individual idiosyncratic behaviours had a place and, akin to a game of trump cards, kids would try out each other's strengths as they continued to try to build a complete game.

Now, allow me to ask you this, how much does your current practice resemble this kind of environment? Does it have that level of commitment to a task? Does it have that kind of vivid visualisation to transport you to another place? Does it mean something to you whether you succeed or fail? What is the consequence depending on the result of the session? Is it pitched at the correct level for your ability – ideally, slightly out of reach? Does it induce the same kind of decision-making and problem-solving processes you experience during a competitive round?

If you have answered yes to all of the above – keep going, you are on a fast track to better golf. If not, let us get down to business.

The older we get, the more we try to convince ourselves that we are smarter than we were when we were kids, in every aspect of our lives. That may be the case in some things, but less so when it comes to how we practise.

As kids, we truly engaged in figuring things out, especially if it was something we liked doing.

Failure never kept us down for long and, in fact, we had an uncanny knack for only remembering the brilliant things we did from an otherwise forgettable game when recalling it to our parents.

However, as adults we veer towards the uninspiring and self-select aspects of our play that confirm a self-fulfilling prophecy about our potential. This thinking moves us away from the aforementioned potent, childlike practice habits, and more towards sterile, mindless, repetitive practice, as if to suggest a perfect form exists, and is attainable only through the pain of monotony.

Why not consider repetition without repetition, akin to what happens on the course?

Apart from when a ball goes out of bounds, we rarely ever hit the same club twice in a row – even the putter is used from a completely different spot on the green every time.

For example, a misfired 8-iron into a par 4 may be the last time you hit that club for an hour. The next hole may be a par 3, the one after that a par 5, and the one after that a short par 4.

Yet, when we convince ourselves that our 8-iron play needs some attention, we will hit 8-iron after 8-iron after 8-iron after 8-iron.

Ignoring one of the most robust findings in skill acquisition called contextual interference, which states that randomising the order of tasks, ie having variability in your practice, carries a greater likelihood of the skills being retained at a later date, and even more so under pressure.

So, rather than hitting 8-irons ad nauseam, with little change from one shot to the next, why not randomly select when you hit an 8-iron and challenge yourself to start from scratch on each shot and apply yourself anew every time.

If you must prevail with the single-club method, this variability can still be infused into your practice by choosing a different target every time, or hitting from a different lie, or attempting a different ball flight.

Apart from the mechanisms that such variability induces at the cognitive processing level, it also prevents the dreaded 'ball drag' effect. This is where players barely change their position from one shot to the next, as they drag ball after ball from the toppled basket – yet another unrealistic behaviour that further reduces the likelihood of their practice transferring to the course.

That is what we see the pros doing, isn't it, so it must be good for our game, mustn't it? Not necessarily.

Social media has a funny way of convincing us that snapshots of practice posted online reflect all the work done elsewhere.

Wrong. In fact, this idea of copying the pros is another fast track to disaster.

When kids see someone doing something that they would like to be able to do themselves, they try it in their own inimitable way. They do not slavishly attempt to identically mimic the action.

Maybe it is because, when we are kids, we understand the fact that we are different from others.

It is a consideration that seems to escape us when we are older as we choose instead to think: I can move in the exact same way (insert name of your favourite player) and when I do, I'm going to get the exact same result. At this point, logic has left the building.

There appears to be a long-standing idea that because golf is a skill-based sport, where even the best players in the world can struggle with their games at times, we need to perfect the skills required to play the game. The problem with this kind of thinking is that when the word perfect comes into the mix, people's practice tends to become more about the minutiae of the game and less about the game itself.

This tendency to work solely on the swing or, worse still, just a small element of the swing in isolation to where that refinement is going to be required, slows the process of your practice transferring to the course even more.

Of course, golf is a technical sport, and so it will benefit from technical refinements from time to time, but even through those days of fine detail work, ensure that the practice is layered with sufficient context and relevance in each shot you play.

This separation of practice from performance that has become so widely accepted does little for the rate of change in your game.

It may get you to where you are going, in time, but surely, our job as coaches and our ambition as players is to get there sooner rather than later.

Consider the following checklist for your practice routines:

- On every shot, do you have a clear target in mind, making sure it is as small and precise as possible?
- Have you allowed the shot to speak to you about what it requires, taking the lie, the weather and any other pertinent information into consideration?
- Finally, are you sure you are looking at the ball as you stand over it, about to pull the trigger?

These are the physical elements of every shot. From a cognitive perspective:

- Have you a context in mind over each shot, like the additional noise that fills your head on the course, such as 'I need to birdie this hole so I have to get it close'?

Of course, the ideal is to not have any such thoughts on the course and robotically go from one shot to the next, hole after hole, with no recollection of what has just happened or what might happen if this unexpected run of good golf continues.

But we are not robots, so let us practise getting better at dealing with the weird and wonderful thoughts that come into our heads when we need them least.

Next, are the shots you are practising relevant to overall performance improvement, or are you practising the shots you are already good at, choosing to avoid the ones that catch you out time and time again?

Does the lion's share of your practice work on your weaknesses, for example your bunker play, your tee shots, your short game?

Or do you give every club and every shot equal attention, regardless of current ability?

Finally, do you have a consequence attached to your practice? If it matters to you when you compete, it should matter to you when you practise. A reward when you do well and succeed on a task, and a penalty when you do not.

Whatever format you play in golf, it is about risk and reward, and the beauty about golf is that it will always give you an opportunity to redeem yourself, because there is always the next shot, the next hole, the next round, the next event.

So choosing to dwell too long in any space is ignoring the opportunity that lies ahead. Thinking that 'I will not leave here until I get 10 in a row' is outdated. Once again, it creates a false positive about your performance.

Set yourself a task, for example a series of up-and-downs from varying distances around a green, and limit yourself to the number of efforts allowed. Regardless of your score at the end, move on to a different task. Learn how to deal with the fact of not succeeding in your practice and being able to move on to other work with a clear head. For the coaches reading this, consider the environment you create for your players to practise in to maximise the likelihood of them getting better.

Is it to fit a model of what you perceive to be the best swing, or is it to work with the player to find the only swing that works for them? Furthermore, does your environment make your players better decision-makers and more competent problem-solvers or does it make them more conscious of their action when all they should be thinking of is the shot in front of them?

Consider asking good enough questions in your session that, should your pupils answer them, they will be improving.

Consider placing problems in front of them. Should they solve them, they will need you less and less as time goes on.

I developed the PEAQ framework to help me stay focussed on my job as a practice coach, to ensure that the work is always about developing players that are more robust.

I Praise a lot. If there is something worthy of praise in a session, I make sure the players hear about it. Otherwise, I say nothing.

I let them Explore as much as possible, making sure I do not get in the way of them figuring things out, allowing them time and space to find their optimal method of engaging with a task – not my way, their way.

I Affirm most of what I see, by connecting the dots of the work done elsewhere as it begins to shine through.

Finally, I work hard on trying to engage through Questions only, resisting the temptation to think that, because I am the coach, I have all the answers.

I want the players I work with to come up with the answers, because there is nothing more empowering than feeling like you have figured something out, you have found a way, and you own your process of getting better. I see golf as a reaction sport that requires players to be adaptable from one shot to the next, so that they can see every shot through fresh eyes, regardless of how a particular hole played the previous day.

For me, practice should always be about developing adaptable players. I believe that when players practise, it should look like and feel like play.

About The Author

Dr Ed Coughlan is a skill acquisition specialist with a particular interest in creating practice environments that challenge players to improve in a way that directly transfers to the competition arena. He also works with coaches interested in developing a more potent space for their players to experience as they push for improvement. He can be followed on Twitter @DrSkillAcq and contacted directly by email on drskillacq@gmail.com.

TRAIN MORE EFFECTIVELY WITH THESE EXERCISES

Here are some games to help your development and keep you entertained, both at the driving range and on the course

Context / ˈkɒntɛkst / Noun. The circumstances that form the setting for an event, statement or action.

TRAINING your ability to adjust and adapt is, in all probability, pretty far removed from your current practice regime. That said, if what you are currently doing isn't exactly helping you set course records, then a radical change may well be just what is required.

Range Training Challenges

Every shot you hit must have some kind of context.

Clearly, shots played on the course all have this, as you will be able to see and, to a degree, measure the outcome relative to your intended target.

You will be able to see if your ball has finished long, short, left, right or in fact adjacent to your target. Did it stay on the fairway or green? Did it come up short or take a big bounce through the back?

Shots played on the range are perhaps not as easy to see or measure unless you are playing to a very clear and specific target.

To help with this, create imaginary greens and fairways in your mind or even between two flags or distance markers on the range.

More often than not, golfers tend to get sucked into direction over distance when hitting shots on the range. Not just weekend golfers but professionals as well.

We remember once observing a young aspiring tour pro on the range one day and asked him what he was aiming at.

"The red flag in the distance," he replied. We then asked how far he was trying to hit the shot.

This was met with a quizzical look. "What do you mean, how far?"

It wasn't a trick question. We merely wanted to know how far he wanted to hit the shot because we knew that distance wasn't a factor he was aware of. Only then did the light bulb switch on. Only then did he realise that he had been paying way more attention to direction over distance.

Our final question was: "Would you ever hit a shot on the golf course without knowing the yardage?"

"I get it – of course not," he replied.'

Golf is a game of distance and direction. One is no good without its counterpart. Please don't fall into the trap of mindlessly aiming at flags with no regard for hitting the shot the appropriate or applicable distance. Think of it along the same lines as you would assessing a putt. There is no point stressing endlessly over the line if you don't get the pace right.

When we were kids, every shot we played on the course or putting green (ranges were pretty thin on the ground and we would much rather play than practise anyway) had some kind of context.

Drives were from the 18th tee at Augusta in our minds, approach shots were to the 18th green on the Old Course and putts were to win the Open.

Did any technical thoughts enter our minds when faced with these shots? Absolutely not. They were all about hitting the fairway, finding the green or holing that winning putt.

1 The Nine Shot Drill

If your existing practice or training regime isn't transferring onto the golf course, it probably doesn't make a whole lot of sense to continue with it.

As a wise old sage once said: "If you always do what you've always done, you'll always get what you always got.'

Rather than beating balls with your favourite club for an hour or working on various moves in your quest to find 'the secret', try this Nine Shot exercise which is a favourite with golf pros the world over. Hit nine different shots with a club you feel most comfortable with. Not nine shots that are the same, one after another, but nine different shots. If you generally hit a fade, hit a high, medium and low fade. Move the ball position around and experiment a little to find the best way for you to hit these shots. Then hit three draws: high, medium and low. Now do the same but your intention this time is to hit three straight shots: high medium and low.

Before you attempt to create any of these shots, make sure you have a very good mental picture of what every one of these shots looks and feels like.

Unfortunately, we can't tell you what any or all of these shots will feel like – because everyone will feel it in their own individual way.

Take a notebook with you and write down what you were thinking and feeling when you successfully created each one of these shots.

Not only will this serve as a reminder of what you were actually doing, it will act as a fantastic reference for when you do this exercise again.

Once you have done it a few times, you will start to see thought and feel patterns form.

In essence, you are creating your very own blueprint for creating each of these nine shots.

You may only need two or three of these different shots on any given day.

However, knowing that you have trained all nine shots means that, if at some point you need to play any of the others, you can play them with confidence and commitment.

The Nine Ball Flights

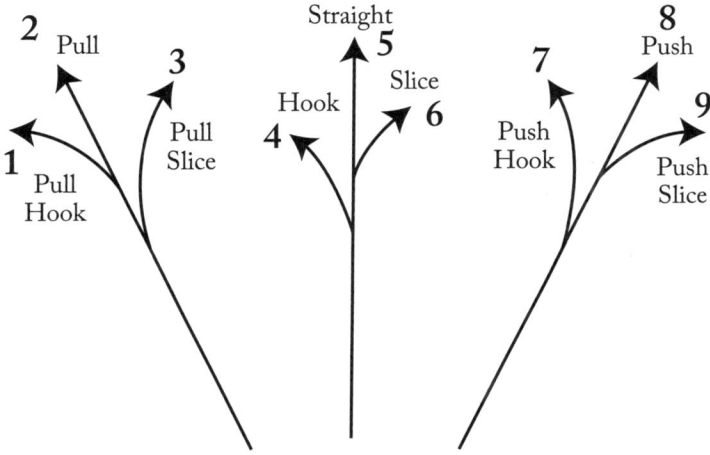

2 The Nine Hole Game

This is a great training exercise and one that works on so many different levels. If you only have a limited amount of time to work on your game, rather than hitting 50 balls with your 7-iron, play the front nine of your home course, or any course for that matter, on the range.

Once you have hit a few shots (there is a world of difference between hitting balls and hitting shots) to warm up, imagine you are standing on the 1st tee. Visualise the 1st hole in your mind and how you would like to play it. Give yourself an imaginary fairway to hit then play the shot with whatever club you believe will give you the desired result.

If it is a driver hole, go to your bag, take the headcover off and play the shot just as you would on the golf course, going through your pre- and post-shot routines.

Great drive! Now you find yourself in the right-hand side of the fairway, 165 yards from the hole which is cut on the left-hand side of the green. You've got a great angle into the flag but the wind is slightly against you and off the left.

Now you have to ask yourself: "What is the shot here and what does that good shot look like?" Is it a high fade with a 5-iron using the wind to help the ball drift into the middle of the green? Or do you feel more comfortable hitting 6-iron, and drawing it against the wind towards that back-left flag? Repeat for the remaining eight holes – or play the full 18 if you have time.

The major benefits include:

a) Becoming absorbed in the task at hand, creating a unique shot in a unique moment in time.

b) Training to play golf, very probably without too much in the way of swing thoughts cluttering up your mind and getting in the way of your creativity.

c) Creating not only shots but an environment which you are going to be in when you next play golf.

d) Being in playing mode before you even get to the 1st tee – something we have achieved to great effect with weekend golfers and tour pros alike.

We hear so many stories about how 'my range game is great but I can't take it to the course'.

It's no wonder, really, when your practice or training and the environment that it happens in bears no resemblance to a golf course.

3 The Intention Game

Stand behind the ball and have the intention to hit a draw. See the ball start slightly to the right and then gently curve back to the target. Then step in and without much conscious thought allow your body to feel the movement that would produce this shape.

Notice how your swing feels. Be aware. Step into the shot and let go. Notice your results. How close do you get to your desired flight?

Then, stand behind the ball and have the intention to hit a fade.

See the ball start slightly to the left and then gently curve back to the target.

Then step in. Again, without much conscious thought allow your body to feel the movement that would produce this shape. Notice how your swing feels. Be aware of the sensations.

What you will be acutely aware of is just how much your intention can influence your movements without you getting too consciously involved. Become interested to see if by changing your intention on the shot you hit you get to bring your swing more into balance.

4 The Three Gears Drill

While so much of what we are discussing here is about more effective training to be ready for the golf course, we would never deny that at times we do need to work at the movements we make in the golf swing and at times it is certainly appropriate to aim to improve these patterns.

The problem is that when you try to change movement patterns you will be battling very hard against what is already there.

Your golf swing is an established pattern of movement and to change it is very difficult. Knowing what you want to change in your swing is very different from knowing how to change it.

A big key to understanding and making progress is to understand the role of speed in the learning process.

If we think of virtually anything in life we have learned to do – like walking or talking – we learned to do it slowly first and then we eventually built up to a natural, non-thinking speed.

Contrast that to how most people approach trying to change their swing. They get some information about the positions they should be in. They then go away and hit balls on the range at normal speed.

At normal speed it is almost impossible to change anything because your brain automatically just reverts to the existing pattern and the 'old' swing comes out.

Many players try to stop the club at certain positions in a drill and then hope this movement will magically appear in the normal swing. This will not happen.

When we do a drill whereby we stop at some point the brain has to create deceleration to hold that position. The problem is that in the normal swing there is no deceleration, just gradual acceleration.

The drill of stopping will not transfer into the normal swing.

The concept of the Three Gears has been one of the most

transformative training drills of all. You may well be wonderfully surprised at the results.

Basically, you get to swing the golf club at a speed where you can really feel the movement and new patterns can be established.

Your brain can lay down new movement pathways as a result of this rich learning environment.

First Gear: In first gear you swing the club at what feels like a ridiculously slow speed. Think about Tai Chi where they make wonderfully slow swirling movements. You swing the club at what feels a very slow speed but you do not stop at any point. You make a continuous motion from start to finish.

You should in effect hit a 'mini shot'. If done correctly the ball will only travel a few yards but it will have all of the characteristics in terms of shape of a good shot. At this speed you will really sense the movement you are trying to make.

It is also a good idea to get your swing on video at this speed as you will more than likely be very encouraged by what you see.

Second Gear: In second gear you swing the club at what feels like 50 per cent of your normal effort and speed. Again this will be interesting as you see the quality of your shots when you take all of the effort out of the motion. Many players report that they hit some of the best shots ever in second gear.

The key is to adopt a spirit of exploration. Allow yourself to have some failures as a pathway to success.

Third Gear: In third gear you swing the golf club with your normal effort and speed. Can you still sense what you are trying to do with the golf club? Does your ability to 'feel' the movement remain the same?

Our recommendation with Three Gears is that you hit shots in blocks of five balls: five balls in first gear, then five balls in second gear, then five balls in third gear. You do not to hit many shots with this process but suddenly the quality of what you are doing in terms of attention is much greater.

If you are going to make swing changes then this is perhaps the key drill. It is very effective use of your time.

5 Consequence Practice

When we look at the game of golf we see that it is the ultimate game of consequence in the sense that every shot you play is accounted for. There is no hiding place on the scorecard. Every time you hit that golf ball there is a consequence in terms of your overall score. So surely, in our training, we should always be building into our plans an element of consequence.

We should also be aiming to replicate as closely as possible the exact requirement of the game itself.

In effect, there is one ball, one unique location, one chance and a score is involved. When we have these specific conditions we are then training for the game itself and not fooling ourselves into thinking that we are getting better.

We need games that give us evidence we are getting better.

One such game that we created many years ago has stood the test of time and is now an established part of golf training at the highest level.

That game is Par 18. Par 18 is a chipping game that will take you roughly 15 minutes to play but will give you a very high-quality workout. You go to the chipping green with one ball, your chipping clubs and your putter. This ball should be the one you play with in tournaments. This is very important as you are training with the ball you are going to play with.

You play from nine unique locations. You play three easy, three medium and three difficult shots. You chip on and you hole out. You go through your full routine as though on the golf course You add up and write down your score against the Par 18. You are only allowed to play this game once in any given day.

Now, just imagine your first score with this game is 24. Not great, but it reflects your current short game ability. However, you stick at this game, you keep playing, you keep working on your skills and a few weeks later that score of 24 has come down to 21. You now know, based on statistics, that you have a better short game.

The more you play this game and the more successful you are at it the more your brain will see a missed green on the golf course as an opportunity. You will have trained yourself to deal with the consequence of the game. The principles of Par 18 can be applied throughout your training.

You are only limited by your imagination. As long as you keep to the key ideas: One ball; one unique location; one chance; score it.

When you embrace consequence practice, you may well find you actually practise less in terms of time but the quality of what you do goes to another level.

6 The TrackMan Combine Test

If you are fortunate enough to have access to a TrackMan and an officially certified operator, the Combine test is a fantastic way not only to highlight any strengths and weaknesses in your game, but also to create the ideal scenario for adjustment and adaptability.

Over and above that, every shot counts towards your total score, so it creates pressure or context as a by-product.

This 60-shot test asks you to hit six shots to 10 different targets – from 60-yard pitches to full-blooded drivers. It then calculates a score out of 100 for each shot, according to how far long, short, left or right your ball carries relative to your intended target. All 60 shots then create a cumulative total score out of 100. We would recommend you do this with three shots to each of the 10 targets and then repeat the process to make up the total of 60 shots.

This way you only have three attempts to hit your ball the correct distance and direction before moving on to the next distance.

The first shot is unlikely to be exactly right for the required distance and direction, therefore allowing you to adjust and adapt for your second attempt. The same goes for your third go at it.

Unless you get it spot on, it's time to adjust and adapt.

One of the great things about this test is that the TrackMan operator will be able to send you the results as an email with all the relevant data including your total score. Be warned, however, if you are at all competitive, which we presume you are, this can become extremely addictive as you will undoubtedly want to beat your previous best every time you take the test.

7 The TrackMan Random Test

Golf is such a random game. It demands that you play a variety of shots of different distances in ever-changing conditions.

Yet so few of us practise, train or prepare for that random element. Creating a random test will allow you to train and prepare for the inevitability of having to hit shots different heights, flights and distances on the golf course.

Once you have identified where your strengths and weaknesses are from the Combine test, you can really start to focus on the distances where you feel you can make big improvements.

Using the TrackMan Performance software, you can set distance parameters – from 125 yards to 195 yards, for example.

You then choose how many shots you want the test to have. We recommend five or 10 shot tests initially. Once the parameters are set, the software will then ask you to hit a shot of a distance between 125 and 195 yards.

Each shot will be to a different distance, ensuring that you have to create a new shot each and every time.

Just like the Combine test, the scores for all your shots will go towards a cumulative total, creating a game-like situation. By using this random format wisely, you are in effect training and preparing for what you know you will face on the course.

On-course Training Challenges

If we could go back in time and speak to an old Scottish professional and tell them we had come up with this 'revolutionary' new idea of training on the golf course they would probably look at us as though we had gone completely mad.

Training on the golf course? Isn't that the most obvious thing to do? Yet it isn't.

Since the relatively recent advent of driving ranges and practice grounds, so many golfers have become more and more removed from the only environment which really matters – the golf course.

Perhaps the reason handicaps stubbornly refuse to come down is because we have become better at practising golf but worse at playing it.

We have become range experts but golf course dummies.

All of the 'on course' training we will share with you is designed to get both your mind and your body ready for the scenarios golf throws up. It is a chaotic game that is never the same one day to the next yet we stand on a range hoping to find that perfect swing that will never let us down. That, we are afraid, is a fantasy.

The reality is that when you play on course a lot of the time you will be fighting your swing. There will be days when you just keep missing green after green.

There will be the times when you become uncomfortable because you have a good score going. There will be the need to be creative. To be able to engage mind and body to create a unique golf shot in a unique location. A golf shot you have never had before and you will never have again.

These training games will get you ready for anything the game can possibly throw at you.

1 The Deliberate Miss Game

If we are going to base our training on the idea that the game of golf will throw various curve balls at you then this game covers so many of those bases.

You will inevitable play rounds of golf where your swing goes off and you start to miss a bunch of greens. There will be days when it seems that your ability to judge your distances is just not there. What are you going to do about it?

Hope that your swing will protect you and you can find some magical swing thought that will shield you from the spectre of poor shots? Good luck with that.

The best thing is to train yourself to be ready for the inevitable chaos that the game will throw at you. To play deliberate miss you have to miss your approach shot deliberately in the best possible spot. So you don't just stand in the fairway and carve your shot anywhere. You get really specific on the very best place to miss the green to give yourself the chance to get up and down.

Paradoxically, as you pick that back left trap, you actually get better at hitting very specific targets and so increase your chance of actually hitting more greens.

You also really get to study the layout of the course. You become much more tuned in to the way a course designer has constructed the course. You play your approach to the best possible area to get up and down.

If you actually hit the green in regulation you have to add one more shot to your score. Miss the green in the best possible location and then see if you can get up and down. Play this game for nine holes and see what kind of score you can put together.

Just imagine the sense of achievement if you can get the ball around nine holes in a good score and you haven't hit a single green.

You will probably not play too many nine holes where you miss all nine greens but if you do you are ready. You have trained for the worst the game can throw at you.

You don't panic when you haven't got your A Game with you.

If, as a scratch player, you can play nine holes with deliberate miss and you are somewhere near one or two over par you know for a fact you can weather any golfing storm that may come your way.

If you are a handicap golfer and you play deliberate miss and you are still close to playing to your handicap for nine holes you really are in business. Play this game regularly and you build mental resilience.

2 The Potential Better Ball Game

An important sensation you need to train for is the discomfort that comes from playing better than you normally do. Strange as it may sound to many, it is a fact of your golfing life that when you play better than normal, when you are well under your handicap you can start to feel a little uneasy.

There is a part of our brain that is more concerned with survival than anything else. One of the ways the ancient part of your brain sees us surviving is if it keeps everything the same. The status quo is predictable. It is a safe haven.

It may seem curious to link this to your golf but the feelings of being outside of your comfort zone are all too real. When you get well under par what is the very best way of returning to your comfort zone? To go right ahead and drop a few shots. Ruins your golf score but at least you feel comfortable again. Sound familiar?

To train yourself for low numbers is essential. To actually see the low numbers on your scorecard. To get used to being in a place that is seemingly better than your normal level of performance.

This is one of the key elements to this game. To actually write your scores on a scorecard. To see the numbers.

Be as real as possible with this. Start with your tee shot and at any point you have the option to play another shot. If your tee shot is fine, then move on.

If your approach is 20 feet from the flag, then see if you can get the next one closer. Knock your next one in closer and then you get a chance to putt. If the first putt misses then you get another go. All the way into the hole.

We have worked with professionals who have shot nine under par for nine holes playing this game and then gone on to shoot some really low scores in tournaments. They have reported the feeling that seeing such low numbers on a scorecard has had a huge impact on their confidence levels.

A number of players have said they have played this game, had some really low numbers but not needed that many second shots. Again, an interesting development for you to explore.

Above all with this training, you are dealing with the feelings the game throws at you and getting yourself ready so that when you have your best game you can really take advantage of it and score much lower.

3 The Three-Club Challenge

One of the great effects of playing with just three clubs is how much creativity you can unleash in your game. You have probably never truly explored just what it is possible to do with a golf club.

Find out what happens when you play the ball back in your stance, when you take loft off, when you put loft on.

How high can you hit a ball with a 4 or 5-iron? What kind of shots can you play with a 7-iron around the green? Can you putt using your 4-iron?

If you consider that one of the greatest players of all time, Seve Ballesteros, learned to play the game with just a 3-iron you can begin to understand why he become such a genius shot-maker.

Seve could play soft-landing bunker shots with that 3-iron or high cut-up pitches. As you learn to play different shots with different clubs you are again getting yourself ready to play the game more creatively with your full set.

You won't always just reach for a certain club on a certain hole like a Pavlovian dog. You will see the uniqueness of this shot in this moment and begin to create shots accordingly.

This game will also reinforce the belief that the 'shot creates the swing' rather than the swing creating the shot.

4 The Worse Ball Game

One of the fundamental principles of training for golf is that a part of your training should be more difficult than the game itself.

Contrast this with how most golfers practise. Standing on a big wide-open field off a perfectly flat lie hitting the same club over and over again is so much easier than the real game to be almost laughable. We practise in that kind of environment then go out onto the golf course to an ever-changing, dynamic, variable and often chaotic challenge and we then wonder why our skills don't transfer. If our practice is always so much easier than the real game, then the real game will always appear difficult to us.

It is the effect of perception. Perception is a key aspect of effective training. If we perceive the game itself to be less challenging than our practice then we set the conditions to really release our true potential. We suggest you play Worse Ball for between six and nine holes. We'll warn you from the outset that this game will drive you a little bit crazy but we promise you in the long run you will really benefit. The frustration will be worth it.

You have to hit two tee shots. If you hit the fairway with one ball and are in the rough with the other, you play the ball in the rough.

Take this principle all the way to the hole.

If you have a six-foot putt for a par and you hole the first putt this doesn't count as a par unless you hole the second putt from the same place.

Worse Ball can be a really frustrating game. You will get angry and upset, you will be annoyed with your score and you will experience a whole bunch of emotions you normally experience on the course.

You are training to deal with the emotional side of the game. The side of the game that if you don't train for then you will pay the price when you come to try to put a score together.

Worse Ball is much harder than the real game so we now get the opposite effect in the sense that if you play this tougher game in practice the real game then seems somewhat easier.

The very opposite of how 99.9 per cent of golfers actually practise.

5 The Forward Tees Game

Virtually all golfers want to hit the ball further, which is fine: there is nothing like the thrill of smashing a long drive.

But if it is scores you are after then it is worth contemplating the fact that no matter how far you hit your tee shots, if you can't finish the hole off then it is of very little value.

To get good at what the great Tony Lema used to call the 'Cone of Contention', the crucial distance from 30 yards up to 100 yards.

We remember many years ago hearing a celebrated national coach tell us the story about what he did with his young players who were only interested in hitting the ball further.

He promised them one day that he was instantly going to get them another 30 to 40 yards closer to the green off the tee to see what effect it would have on their scoring. Suddenly they were all ears to find out the secret to longer drives. He then threw them a curve ball and told them the extra 30 yards would come from playing off the forward tees. They played 18 holes and, to a man, the scoring hardly improved. He had highlighted graphically that more distance without a good wedge game is pointless.

This game will require you to swallow a little bit of your pride but it will really show you the state of your wedge game. At the very least it will give you the opportunity of playing more wedges in the golf course environment. Go out and play off the forward tees. See how your scoring matches up.

This game will provide you with such valuable feedback. Notice your patterns with your wedges are you generally short or long? Left or right? Note down the patterns.

If your scoring is not significantly better playing off the forward tees then driving distance is not your issue.

6 The No-Pin Golf Game

According to Dr Riccio, the single most important statistic if you want to reduce your scoring and become a better golfer is your GIR stat. Your ability to hit more Greens in Regulation is perhaps the biggest weapon into your lower score armoury.

In a nutshell, if you can hit on average one more green in regulation your handicap will reduce roughly by a corresponding shot. Obviously this statistic is not definitive for everyone but we have found that when you get a jump in GIR you will be pleasantly surprised by your results. You will gain some powerful momentum in the quest for improvement.

So far so good. Most golfers armed with this information would think it is all about getting a better, more accurate, golf swing –which in part may be true. But we have found a training game that can transform your GIR stat without doing anything to your swing.

Let's first of all get the best out of what we currently have before we go in search of swing perfection. Most golfers miss a lot of greens because of where they aim.

The flag is hypnotic. Players of all levels end up in the most horrendous of situations on the course because they shoot at the pin tucked back left or front right. Miss your shot even slightly and you can be in big trouble. However, when your target is the middle/widest part of the green you have a different margin for error. No-Pin Golf is exactly what it says.

First of all, find out what your current GIR stat is. Then go out and play some nine-hole stretches on your course where the pin doesn't exist. No matter what club you have in your hand your job is to hit the middle of the green. Every single green in regulation is a little victory.

Take note of what this does to your averages in terms of greens hit and, perhaps more importantly, your actual scoring.

You can then play No-Pin Golf in actual tournaments.

Depending on your ability level No-Pin may start at a different level of your set. If you are a high-handicapper, you may play No-Pin with all of your clubs. For a scratch golfer, No-Pin may start at 5-iron and upwards.

The great beauty of this kind of training is you get to find out what makes you tick as a unique individual.

7 The Irons Only Challenge

This is another great game to play on the course to get you out of what we call auto-pilot thinking.

So many times when we play the same course over and over again we just become like a robot and pull out a certain club on a certain hole because that is the way we have always done it.

We end up having a 'bogey hole' and yet time and again we see golfers with this issue keep using the same club off the tee.

One of the most important things to do with a negative repeating pattern is to break it. By playing iron-only off all of the tees you then get to play a different golf course. You break the limiting patterns of familiarity. Yes, you may well be going in with your second shot from way back but we promise you that you will see you can still get the job done. The game forces you to think differently. You may have to sharpen your short game and your wedge play but, again, you are practising this in the context of the golf course.

You are in the real situation of finding a way to get the job done.

You are on the golf course training yourself to really look at the hole you are playing as opposed to blindly following some kind of existing script.

Be creative. Have fun putting a score together and seeing your own familiar course in a much different light.

8 The Fairways and Greens Game

One of the best ways to lower your scores and become a better player is paradoxically not to become too obsessed with the actual score itself but to become immersed in the processes that will create the best foundation to allow a score to emerge.

Clearly, hitting more fairways and greens is desirable so let's train our brain to become more focussed on these very processes.

The Fairways and Greens game is ridiculously simple but profoundly effective.

By giving yourself one point for every fairway you hit and two points for every green you hit in regulation you get to train your attention. Instead of just standing on the tee and smashing the ball anywhere into the blue yonder we perhaps get to play a little bit more within ourselves. Find the fairway. Somehow.

Even if it is not your Sunday-best shot, every single fairway you hit sets you up to then hit the green.

As you play your approach, the two points are not dependent on knocking it close to the pin. You get two points regardless of where the ball ends up as long as it ends up on the green.

This game ties in perfectly with No-Pin golf. You really tune in to getting the ball on the putting surface. The two points FEEL good. You are also training for what you can do in tournaments when you maybe get a bit too score-orientated. Instead of getting ahead of yourself, just come back into the here and now and hit this fairway. Then hit this green. The idea of playing one shot at a time is the oldest cliche in the book but it is still very relevant. However again as we keep making the point this mindset has to be trained. It will not happen automatically.

The fairways and greens points game gets you absorbed into a process that will create the very best foundations for great scoring.

The great scores will sneak up on you as a result of effective training.

9 The Half-Set Challenge

In a world where we have clubs designed to do everything but hit the ball for us in the form of hybrids, lob wedges (none of which incidentally come with a user's manual) we have lost the ability or necessity to create different or relevant shots.

Those of us who were fortunate to learn to play the game as kids probably only had a few odd, cut-down old clubs or a half-set at best. Consequently, we learned to play a variety of shots with the clubs we had. We learned how to hit low, chasing draws to get a bit of extra distance. We learned how to play greenside bunker shots with a 9-iron. We learned how to be creative and how to have fun.

Why don't you and your regular playing companions arrange to play a Half-Set Challenge'? We'd love to hear your feedback. We're pretty confident you will all have tremendous fun doing it and you might even be surprised at how well you play.

10 The Wrong-Club Challenge

This is basically a variation on playing with a half-set. The only difference being, you are allowed to have the maximum of 14 clubs in your bag. However, if you normally hit driver off the 1st, you must use a 3-wood, hybrid or a long iron. If your second shot would normally be the distance where you would reach for your 6-iron, you have to create a shot with a 5 or 7-iron.

If you normally reach for your 60-degree wedge from a greenside bunker, use a less-lofted wedge and you'll have to open up the face to create the shot required.

You can carry this on to the greens if you like but please, please don't be trying to pitch it into the hole off beautifully cut and prepared greens. We do not want the greenkeepers of the world knocking on our doors. It's probably safer to use the skills you have learned from reading our first book The Lost Art Of Putting.

Try this once in a while to get your creative juices flowing and unleash your natural shotmaking skills.

11 The Play It Again Game

This is one of the few exercises where we would actively encourage you to hit two consecutive shots from the same place to the same target.

If the first one doesn't quite match up to your intention, visualisation and expectation, make a small adjustment with the second shot to create your desired outcome.

If your first shot does indeed match up to your intended outcome, well done. No second shot required.

If you do use this exercise on the course, please choose a quiet time and place and be respectful of other golfers.

COACHING, PRACTICE HABITS AND THE FUTURE OF GOLF

Markus Westerberg, a PGA professional, psychologist and author, explains why the game is thriving in Sweden

GOLF has been in decline in most parts of the world for over a decade. Memberships and the number of played rounds have diminished. Golf clubs are closing. Could coaching and golfers' practice habits be a part of this? Studies from Sweden suggest so. A golfer's skill level is closely related to whether they quit or not.

Sweden is known for Vikings, skiing and tall blondes. But since the late 1990s, golf has become synonymous with the country. With superstars like Annika Sörenstam and Henrik Stenson and over 10 per cent of the population playing more than four rounds per year, Sweden is a golfing nation.

In a world where golf participation is in decline, the Swedes are swimming against the stream. Here, memberships are actually on the rise for four straight years. What is Sweden doing to have this success? The answer could be found in the heart of coaching, in the Swedish PGA.

Is Skill Golf's Saviour?
Golf is a difficult game. It takes time to learn and if you don't reach

a certain level you are likely to quit. Actually, if you stay with too high a handicap for too long, the odds are that you won't find golf worth the time and the money.

One survey found that the reason for the decline in memberships wasn't attracting new golfers. It was keeping them in the game. During Sweden's recess years (yes, Sweden has had the same problem as so many other nations) there was a constant flow of new golfers. The problem was that they weren't staying in the game and a major contributor was that they were playing too badly.

One study, on the importance of playability, was released in 2007 and in 2010 the Swedish PGA launched their new coaching programme with an emphasis on holistic coaching. The message was clear: We need to make golfers better for the sake of the game.

So how did this new focus reflect on the coaching? First of all, the Swedish PGA's coaches' programme has a strong emphasis on what happens to the golf ball rather than the looks of the golf swing or the putting stroke. All coaches learn that controlling the golf ball is the ultimate judge of a golf swing's proficiency. This may sound like kicking against an open door, but as a reader of this book you will know that it isn't. The golfing world is full of mechanics who leave golfers confused instead of competent.

Furthermore, research shows that an over-emphasis on the movement itself leads to worse performances, inefficient learning and, moreover, it is a component of choking.

The aforementioned scientific approach was another update by the Swedes as they incorporated the "psychology of learning and performance" into their programme. To make golfers better, practice has to count. The psychology of learning and performance sometimes challenges traditional doctrines. I have already mentioned the common misconception of correcting a golf swing on the basis of its looks instead of the results it produces.

Another fallacy is taking performance in practice for learning. How well you perform in practice is not a sign of learning and in order to improve as a golfer, you need to learn. Learning means how well you perform afterwards. How well you retain your skills from the practice tee to the golf course. And, again, playing well on the golf course is what keeps golfers in the game.

In order to improve your learning you should change clubs and targets when you practice on the driving range. Often! Preferably, on every shot. It also means that you should practice putting with one ball and never repeat a putt.

How did this challenge traditional doctrines? When you think performance in practice is a sign of improvement, you will repeat the same shots and putts over and over because it is easier.

You will also arrange practice to hit good shots rather than challenge yourself. Performance in practice is a trap.

The perfect analogy to this is gym training. In the gym you make practice harder to get stronger. You leave the gym weaker than when you got there. That is why you put weights on the bar. You add load to improve. The same holds true for your golf game.

Coaching For The Future

Life isn't black or white. There are certainly many reasons why Swedish golf is not in recess and Swedish coaches weren't completely blue-eyed before the reform of 2010. But there has been a shift in Sweden. Golf is on the rise and good coaching has contributed. When you enter a difficult game like golf, you need to get off on the right track. You need to know true cause and effect so that you don't get entangled in the myriad of good tips.

The reason why you topped your approach was that your clubhead was too high up at impact. There are no other causes.

The most common belief is that the reason for a top is you didn't keep your eyes on the ball. Now, this could have contributed, but keeping your eyes on the ball is not a guaranteed solution to your topping problem.

A guaranteed solution is learning to land the clubhead in the right spot – ie brushing the grass after the golf ball. Nothing else. This is the kind of coaching that makes you a better golfer and, as you know now, getting better isn't only a personal journey. It is for the sake of the game.

And if you still don't believe me on the topping thing, take a look at Annika's head and Henrik's head at impact. Their blue eyes have left the ball well before their club has hit it.

About The Author
Markus Westerberg, from Sweden, is a PGA club professional and a qualified psychologist. He is the author of The Golfer's Sixth Sense – How the unconscious mind runs the show. A former tournament professional, Markus is a renowned coach and acts as a consultant to the Swedish PGA education programme.
Find out more at **markuswesterberg.com**

OUR
CONCLUSIONS

W E have reached the end of our time together but we hope
this is the start of some wonderful golfing experiences for
you in the future. As we have reflected throughout the book, the
time we have is precious. We only have so many Tuesdays left and
in a sense we all suffer from a protective human delusion that we
will keep going and going and there will always be another chance,
another week to 'get it right', more time to work on our game.

Unfortunately, this is not the case. We had a very sad email from
one of our clients who had suggested to one of his friends he should
get a copy of The Lost Art of Putting. His friend had called him
to say the book had arrived and he looked forward to gaining some
insight for his struggles on the greens. The next communication
was from his friend's wife who informed him that her husband had
suddenly and shockingly passed away. No more Tuesdays.

We don't say this to draw a veil of gloom over the conclusion to
this hopefully optimistic book but to reinforce the idea that the
time to do what you really want to do is now. Don't let the clock
beat you. Of course, not one of us has control of our entry and our

exit from this world but we do have control over what we attend to while we are here.

The auto-pilot of habitual patterns and habits is so incredibly strong for human beings. It's the pull of the familiar, the ties that bind. They are all incredibly strong. Yes, we can continue to live our lives with the pull of the familiar or we can step back and ask some deeper questions about how we are best going to use the time we have left.

If what you have been doing with your game has not made you a happier golfer, if you feel that all the work you are putting in isn't giving you much reward, then maybe it is time to look at changing your approach. To take a different direction.

We have not prescribed exactly what to do in this book, we have not given you formulas. That is up to you.

What we have given you is a series of ideas and options to try out. We are not interested in debating where the club should be in the downswing or who has the better 'method'. That debate has been exhausted to the point of irrelevance. It is also an approach that puts the coach at the centre of the equation instead of the player.

For us, it is about you seeing what you have inside of your unique body and mind.

What could you achieve if you set yourself free to play a game that you decided to play. If you played the game you had decided to play as opposed to the one the media and society had dictated to you?

We are not for one minute saying competition and winning is not important – after all, we have both built our careers around trying to help people improve their scoring – but it is not the whole picture.

The way to lower your scores is not just about a certain position in the swing. It is about your relationship to the whole game.

The whole complex interaction between you, an individual, who is a little bit different every day and a golf course which is different every day. It is not the ever-elusive consistency you should be looking for – that is a fool's errand. It is the ability to adapt to the questions you will be asked today with the tools you have available today. The ability to be resilient and steadfast in the face of the uncertainty the game constantly throws at you. To be at peace with the uncertainty. To come out on the other side and embrace the idea of creating golf shots is incredibly liberating and such good fun.

To create a shot in your mind's eye and then trust your body to organise the movement to make that happen is a joyful experience in and of itself. Of course you are not going to hit good shots all of the time, we have stressed this to you over and over again.

But when you embrace the possibility this shot – this unique shot in this unique moment – could be a good shot then you create a spark in yourself. You can ignite a new passion for the game you may have thought you had lost forever. That is the art of playing the game of golf.

In a world drowning in information and technical overload we may just need the game of golf more than ever. To be able to get away from your devices for a while and just let the world slow down a little. To connect back to the inherent joy of being in and observing the outside world.

To be in that world as a direct personal, lived experience as opposed to a vicarious secondary-screen experience seen through someone else's lens.

That is The Lost Art of Golf – and maybe to an extent the lost art of living life.

To find some insights through your own personal and first-hand experience on the golf course may just open a door to other areas in your life where the ability to be present and to be able to create may become extremely valuable.

We have enjoyed the experience of being absorbed in the creation of this book. At times when writing, time does seem to stand still and your thoughts flow. Other days it can just seem hard work and the thoughts and ideas come less easily.

The key we have found is to stay with your commitment. In spite of distractions and sometimes unwanted feelings you stay with the process that at times may feel like it is leading nowhere.

Then, if you hold with your commitment, if you ride the inevitable ups and downs and if you keep on a path of exploration, all of a sudden, the commitment results in sentences leading to chapters which eventually add up to what you have just read as a book.

Not unlike the game of golf we have been attempting to explore.

We have been lucky to enlist the help of some great people on this journey and we know their help and guidance has added much to our own understanding. We are going to keep exploring what could be possible and we do sincerely hope you will stay with us on this journey and connect back with the Lost Art of Playing Golf.

All the very best,
Gary and Karl

THE LOST ART OF GOLF SERIES

Learn more about the Lost Art of Golf series at:
thelostartofgolf.com

• Be the first to find out about our latest work

• Introduce yourself to The Lost Art of Putting

• Purchase The Lost Art of Putting

• Read Karl and Gary's regular blogs

• Listen to our series of podcasts

• Watch our latest instructional videos

• Contact the authors

Twitter: **@LostArtofGolf**